TIMELY TRUTHS FROM THE
BOOK OF
MORMON

TIMELY TRUTHS FROM THE
BOOK OF MORMON

ALLAN K. BURGESS

Bookcraft
Salt Lake City, Utah

Library of Congress Catalog Card Number: 95–80717

ISBN 1-57008-199-9

First Printing, 1995

Printed in the United States of America

CONTENTS

Chapter One

BECOMING HIGHLY FAVORED OF THE LORD
1 Nephi 1–2

Afflictions Have Little to Do with Whether We Are Blessed

In the very first verse of the Book of Mormon, Nephi begins to teach us about the wonderful blessings of God. He states: "Having seen many afflictions in the course of my days, *nevertheless*, having been highly favored of the Lord in all my days . . ." He goes on to say that he has received great knowledge of the goodness of God and of the mysteries of God.

At first reading someone might wonder how a person could have many afflictions and yet be highly favored of the Lord. In Nephi's case he is not exaggerating when he states that he suffered many afflictions. He was the victim in a murder plan on five different occasions—four of these by his own brothers. He left his comfortable home, spent eight years in a hot, barren desert, suffered persecution and ridicule. Yet he felt that he was highly favored because, through these afflictions, he came to know God and learn of his mysteries, which are learned through the promptings of the Holy Ghost. Nephi considered anything that brought him closer to God to be a blessing, and so it was.

This same insight and perspective is demonstrated by many

members of the Church today. One such person was a Hawaiian member named Joe Kekahuna. Shortly after Elder Cantwell started serving his mission in Hawaii his companion told him they were going to visit Brother Kekahuna, who was a patient in a leper hospital in Pearl City.

Elder Cantwell was deeply worried about the visit for fear that he would contract the disease, but his companion assured him that leprosy was not as contagious as many supposed. As Elder Cantwell walked into Joe's room his apprehensions returned, for Joe's body was in an advanced stage of deterioration. Elder Cantwell's heart was filled with pity, and he had no idea what he should say or do. Joe sensed his apprehension and uncertainty:

> "Don't feel sorry for me, Elder," he said. "I am a dying man, but I am a happy man, too. When I was young, like you, I thought I would live forever. I did bad things. I was a hard man, who would never listen to the missionaries. I liked my good time; I had no place in my life for God. This disease sent me to Molokai, to Kalaupapa, where I lived among the lepers. I found God in Kalaupapa, and I found the Church."
>
> His voice broke with emotion as he continued, "I'm glad I have this disease. Without it, I would be the same as I was, and there would be no future for me. I would have lost everything. Learn from me, elder. Learn from Joe Kekahuna, the leper." (Lee G. Cantwell, *Ensign*, January 1994, pp. 65–66.)

An important step in receiving the blessings of God is to turn toward God in time of opposition and affliction. It is helpful to remember that God has created a world of opposition, for trial and tribulation are necessary for soul growth. God has never promised us a life free from hardship, but he has promised us such things as direction, guidance, peace, and understanding during this life, and eternal life (godhood) in the life to come. As both Nephi and Joe Kekahuna testify, there are no physical blessings that compare to eternal life and the blessings of the Spirit.

The Greatest Blessing of God Is Eternal Life

Through diligent prayer and a desire to do the will of God, Lehi learned many great and marvelous things. He shared one of these things when he exclaimed to the Lord: "Thy power, and goodness, and mercy are over all the inhabitants of the earth; and because thou art merciful, thou wilt not suffer those who come unto thee that they shall perish!" (1 Nephi 1:14.) Verse fifteen states that his "soul did rejoice, and his whole heart was filled, because of the things which he had seen, yea, which the Lord had shown unto him."

It is no wonder that his soul rejoiced, for there is no greater blessing God can give us than to know that we will not perish but can live with him again. Immortal life in God's presence is referred to as eternal life, and God has told us that it is the greatest of all of his gifts (see D&C 14:7).

Because we live in a world that promotes immediate gratification, it is easy to get caught up in the challenges of the moment and forget the great blessing that we are working for. The reward of eternal life works exactly the opposite of most things the world promotes. Worldly things can be enjoyed now and paid for later. But eternal life is something that we purchase each day through our obedience but do not receive until some time after we leave this life. By focusing daily on this goal of eternal life we can keep an eternal perspective that will allow us to keep things of lesser importance from robbing us of this great blessing.

God Can Bless Us With the Power to Surmount Our Problems

Even though eternal life is a future blessing, there are many blessings that are available to us daily, here and now. Of the Jews' attempt to take Lehi's life, Nephi wrote: "They also sought his life, that they might take it away. But behold, I, Nephi, will show unto you that the tender mercies of the Lord are over all those whom he hath chosen, because of their faith, to make them mighty even unto the power of deliverance." (1 Nephi 1:20.)

Have you noticed that, throughout these chapters, Nephi is using his father's story to teach gospel principles that affect the lives of all of us? In this particular verse he doesn't say that because of Lehi's faith Lehi was delivered, but he indicates that all of us can receive this blessing if we will gain the faith Lehi had. All of us know that God does not deliver us from every physical danger and handicap that we face, but numerous times every day God does pour out physical blessings upon the faithful. And God has promised us that, when we are faithful, he will always deliver us from spiritual harm. Paul taught that "God . . . will not suffer you to be tempted above that ye are able; but will with the temptation also make a way to escape, that ye may be able to bear it" (1 Corinthians 10:13). We can be assured that, as we place our faith and trust in God and strive to do the things he desires of us, he will give us the strength to overcome sin and temptation in our lives. What physical blessing can compare to receiving the power to overcome our sins?

Blessings Come from Doing the Will of God

The Lord spoke to Lehi and said, "*Blessed* art thou Lehi, because of the things which thou hast *done*" (1 Nephi 2:1). The gospel of Jesus Christ promises great blessings, but they only come to us as we *obey* the gospel, *keep* the commandments, and *do* the will of our Heavenly Father. Lehi was blessed of the Lord because he was "obedient unto the word of the Lord" and "did as the Lord commanded him" (1 Nephi 2:3). Our faith in the Lord is demonstrated much more by what we do than by what we say. The importance of both faith and doing the will of God is illustrated in the following story (heard by the author at a stake conference in February 1994).

Some years ago there was a young boy who stuttered so badly that he could not even communicate his name. His parents took him to the best speech specialists, but none of them could help him. When he was thirteen years old his father felt that he might receive help through a patriarchal blessing. The patriarch blessed him that his disability would be removed from him so that he could serve a powerful mission where he would be able to express himself.

When he turned mission age, he still had his physical disability. He had never given a talk or blessed the sacrament or been able to express himself vocally. When the bishop issued the mission call he only accepted through faith. It is difficult to comprehend the faith it would take to leave for the mission field knowing you could not even verbally express your name.

When the mission president met with the boy, he realized something would have to change or he would have to send him home. The elder was assigned to a veteran missionary who only had one month left on his mission. They went tracting and decided to take turns at the doors. When it was the young elder's turn, he couldn't even express who he was. While he was sweating with embarrassment and looking at the ground, the woman said, "Well, what do you want? Speak up!" His companion talked to the woman and never went tracting with the elder again.

Many would not have had the faith to continue in the face of these and similar problems, but this young man refused to give up. After all, God had asked him to serve a mission and promised him the power to do so. Through much pleading with the Lord and exercising of his great faith, this young man began to overcome his speech condition. He became a powerful speaker and teacher. Since that time he has served in many key positions in the Church, including ten years as a stake president. He is currently spreading the gospel of Jesus Christ throughout the world.

The great healing power and the power to preach the gospel came to this young man because of his powerful faith and dedicated obedience. The importance of obedience in receiving the help of the Lord was taught by President Heber J. Grant when he stated:

> There is but one path of safety to the Latter-day Saints, and that is the path of duty. It is not a testimony, it is not marvelous manifestations, it is not knowing that the Gospel of Jesus Christ is true, . . . it is not actually knowing that the Savior is the Redeemer, and that Joseph Smith was His prophet, that will save you and me, but it is the keeping of the commandments of God, the living the life of a Latter-day Saint. (*Improvement Era*, November 1936, p. 659.)

True Happiness Has Little to Do with Physical Possessions

That happiness is not a matter of earthly possessions is taught well by the prophet Lehi, who left his land and gold and silver and all of his precious things and dwelt in a tent in the wilderness. After traveling three days in the wilderness, Lehi built an altar and gave thanks to God for all of his blessings. As we look around us we see people with nice homes who are not satisfied. They want a home that is newer or bigger or better. They have dependable transportation but they desire something new and sleek—something with power windows and four-speed window wipers. No matter how many physical blessings they enjoy, they are dissatisfied and unhappy. In their misguided attempt to gain happiness, they overlook the true source of happiness: understanding the things of God and keeping his commandments. This truth has never been demonstrated better than in the lives of Nephi, Laman, and Lemuel.

Laman and Lemuel constantly murmured. They complained that they had to live in the wilderness. They were upset that they had to leave their riches and comforts behind. As far as we can tell they were dissatisfied and unhappy all of their lives. Why didn't they accept their father as a prophet? Why didn't they believe that Jerusalem would be destroyed? Why didn't they gain the spiritual blessings that came to Lehi, Nephi, and Sam? The answer is given in 1 Nephi 2:12, which states: "And they did murmur because they knew not the dealings of that God who had created them." They could not be happy because they never came to trust and understand God and, therefore, keep his commandments.

The next question that might be asked is why? Why didn't they come to know the dealings of God? Nephi explains: "[Lehi] spake many great things unto them, which were hard to be understood, save a man should inquire of the Lord; and they being hard in their hearts, therefore they did not look unto the Lord as they ought" (1 Nephi 15:3). When Nephi asked of them if they had inquired of the Lord concerning the things Lehi taught, they answered, "We have not; for the Lord maketh no such thing known unto us" (1 Nephi 15:9).

Nephi's story, just the opposite of his brothers', demonstrates to us how we can know the workings of God and receive his blessings. Nephi, having great desires to know the mysteries of God, cried unto the Lord seeking that knowledge. His heart was softened so that he believed all the words of his father. The Lord spoke to him, saying:

"Blessed art thou, Nephi, because of thy faith, for thou hast sought me diligently, with lowliness of heart. And inasmuch as ye shall keep my commandments, ye shall prosper, and shall be led to a land of promise; yea, even a land which I have prepared for you; yea, a land which is choice above all other lands." (1 Nephi 2:19–20.)

Although the land of promise mentioned above specifically refers to the American continents, we can think of it as referring also to the celestial kingdom, which indeed is a land that is choice above all other lands.

Conclusion

Sometimes we make things more complicated than they are. As Alma told his son Helaman, "Let us not be slothful because of the easiness of the way" (Alma 37:46). The formula for receiving God's blessings is simple. As Nephi taught throughout these two chapters, it consists of learning the word of God, praying sincerely, and diligently striving to keep the commandments of God. Laman and Lemuel refused to follow these steps and became unhappy and unsuccessful in life. Nephi and Sam followed this process and received peace, direction, power, and rejoicing in this life and eternal life in the world to come. These same blessings will come to us as we study the scriptures, talk with our Heavenly Father, and strive to do his will.

Chapter Two

"IT FILLED MY SOUL WITH EXCEEDINGLY GREAT JOY"
1 Nephi 8, 11–12

Why Study the Tree of Life Vision?

Lehi's vision of the tree of life represents this life and explains what we need to do in order to partake of eternal life and the joy that our Father has prepared for us. It also illustrates the great happiness we can obtain during this life as we partake of the Savior's atonement. As we study this vision, we can evaluate our own progress meaningfully and determine where we are in our quest for eternal life.

What the Symbols Represent

A brief explanation of what the symbols represent should provide a good base for discussing the four types of people depicted in the dream.

The tree of life and the fruit of the tree (1 Nephi 8:10–12; 11:21–23; 15:36). After Nephi saw in vision the conception and birth of Jesus, the angel said, "Behold the lamb of God, yea, even the Son of the Eternal Father! Knowest thou the meaning of the tree which thy father saw?"

Nephi answered: "Yea, it is the love of God, which sheddeth itself abroad in the hearts of the children of men; wherefore, it is the most desirable above all things."

The angel responded, "Yea, and the most joyous to the soul."

The tree represents more than just the love of God in general. It symbolizes the greatest manifestation of God's love, which is the gift of Jesus and his atonement. Jesus explained to Nicodemus, "God so loved the world, that he gave his only begotten Son, that whosoever believeth in him should not perish, but have everlasting life" (John 3:16).

Through the atonement of Jesus, God offers his love to all his children on the earth. As we obey the laws and ordinances of the gospel, we partake of the tree (atonement) and receive "peace in this world, and eternal life in the world to come" (D&C 59:23).

There is no joy in this life that compares to the blessings that come through forgiveness of sin and peace of soul. When King Benjamin's people pleaded with God to apply the atoning blood of Christ in their lives, the Spirit came upon them and they received peace of conscience and remission of sins, which filled their hearts with joy. Eventually, the greatest fruit of the Atonement—eternal life— becomes available to all those who continue to repent and keep God's commandments.

The tree of life has been a symbol of Jesus and his atonement from the time of Adam and Eve. It was the tree in the midst of the Garden of Eden whose fruit contained the power of everlasting life (see Genesis 2:9; 3:22–24). John the Revelator wrote the words he heard in the great revelation: "To him that overcometh will I give to eat of the tree of life, which is in the midst of the paradise of God" (Revelation 2:7). Our whole purpose in coming to this earth is to so live that we may partake of the tree of life.

The strait and narrow path. The path that leads to the tree is a strait and narrow one. The Lord revealed that "strait is the gate, and narrow the way that leadeth unto the exaltation and continuation of the lives, and few there be that find it" (D&C 132:22). The word *strait* means narrow or restricted. Nephi taught that repentance and baptism are the gate that admits us to the strait and narrow path (see 2 Nephi 31:17–18). Therefore the only people who are on the path to the tree are those who are members of the Lord's true Church.

To get on the path is not enough. To stay there we need to live the gospel of Jesus Christ and partake of the saving ordinances of the gospel. Elder Boyd K. Packer has said of these ordinances: "They are more than advisable or desirable, or even necessary. More, even, than essential or vital, they are *crucial* to each of us. . . . "Now, I counsel you to take inventory of your spiritual progress. Is your life in order? Have you received the ordinances of the gospel that you should possess by this time in your life? Are they valid? If they come under the influence of the sealing power and authority, they will remain intact eternally; and your life, to this point, is in proper order." (*BYU 1980 Devotional Speeches of the Year,* pp. 12–13.)

The rod of iron (1 Nephi 8:19–20, 24; 11:25; 15:23–24). Lehi noticed in his dream that a rod of iron extended along the strait and narrow path that led to the tree of life. The iron rod represents the word of God—the ordinances and teachings of the gospel of Jesus Christ. Only by following these ordinances and teachings can we partake of the sweet fruit of the tree.

When we cling or hold fast to the word of God (by learning and obeying it) and press forward along the path, Satan and his temptations have no power over us. The rod is made of iron, thus representing the strength and firmness the gospel can give us as we face the temptations and challenges that are part of this mortal existence.

The large and spacious building (1 Nephi 8:26–28; 11:35–36; 12:18). The building represents the pride and wisdom of the world. If we get caught up in worldly knowledge and possessions, we become proud and lack the meekness and humility that is needed to understand the word of God. The vision shows that it is impossible to be filled with pride and still hold on to the iron rod. In Lehi's vision the spacious building falls, just as all those who value the things of the world over the things of God will fall.

The mists of darkness (1 Nephi 8:22–24; 12:17). These represent the temptations of the devil. If we do not have a firm hold on the word of God, the temptations that buffet us will blind us to the truth and harden us to the prompting of the Spirit. If this happens we wander onto broad roads and are lost.

The river of filthy water (1 Nephi 8:13; 12:16; 15:26–29). The river represents the filthiness of sin and the depths of hell. Those who have not been cleansed by partaking of the fruit (atonement of Jesus) remain unclean and, at death, their spirits go to the spirit prison or to hell. Here they suffer guilt and agony for their sins insofar as they do not repent and benefit from the cleansing atonement of Christ.

Four Types of People

Many have compared the groups of people in Lehi's dream (see 1 Nephi 8) to the four types of individuals depicted in the parable of the soils (see Matthew 13:3–23). In both of these accounts the emphasis seems to be on four general types of receptivity to the word of God. As we discuss each group of people identified in Lehi's dream, we will also indicate what seems to be the parallel group found in the parable of the soils and will suggest and discuss its characteristics. This will afford the reader the opportunity, on the basis of the interpretations, to determine the group into which he currently fits and to make the necessary changes if that group is not the one headed for eternal life.

Group One

Lehi saw "numberless concourses of people, many of whom were pressing forward, that they might obtain the path which led unto the tree." These people actually commenced in the path, which suggests that they joined the Church of Jesus Christ and began the journey along the path leading to eternal life.

However, "an exceedingly great mist of darkness" arose (trials, temptations), as a result of which these people lost their way, wandered from the path, and were lost. In the parable of the soils, the soil represents a person's heart and thus his or her receptivity to the word of God. In this parable these people are represented by stony ground—ground with bedrock covered by a few inches of soil. Like those in Lehi's dream, these people accepted the word with gladness but put down no depth of root. When tribulation or persecution or temptation came along, they were offended and separated themselves from the word of God.

Our wards contain many people who have been baptized members of the Church but for numerous reasons have left the strait and narrow path and are no longer actively involved in the Lord's kingdom. These people, who are referred to as less active, need our assistance in re-sparking their testimonies and developing deeper spiritual roots.

Anyone can fall into this category if he or she stops doing those things that bring spiritual growth, such as prayer, scripture study, church attendance, and gospel service. When a person's activity in these areas slows down, his grasp on the iron rod weakens. When a problem that tests his faith comes along, he does not have a sufficient hold on the word of God, and he lets go and loses his way. This does not usually happen all at once but takes place over a period of time until any supposed offense or problem may cause the person to leave the path. In the scriptures this is referred to as dwindling in unbelief.

Group Two

Lehi saw many people who caught hold of the rod of iron and did "press forward through the mist of darkness, clinging to the rod of iron" until they partook of the fruit of the tree of life. These people repented of their sins, were baptized into the Church, and tasted the sweet joy of peace and forgiveness.

Then Lehi noticed a large and spacious building that was filled with people who were in the "attitude of mocking and pointing their fingers towards" those who were partaking of the tree. At this, the people who had partaken of the fruit became ashamed because of those who were scoffing at them, and they fell away from the path. The angel told Nephi that the great and spacious building represents the worldly wisdom, the vain imaginations, and the pride of the children of men (see 1 Nephi 12:18).

This group of people may compare to those in the parable of the soils who accept and live the word of God but allow riches, lusts, and worldly pleasures to begin to grow in their lives. These thorns and weeds begin to choke out the things of God until no good fruit can be produced. The fruits of the Spirit are "love, joy, peace, longsuffering, gentleness, goodness, faith, meekness, temperance" (Galatians 5:22–23). These godly attributes cannot grow in an atmosphere of pride, lust, and worldly desires.

Many of these people still attend church and participate in some aspects of gospel living, but so many other interests have taken priority in their lives that they no longer feel the joy and the excitement of the gospel. Their grasp of the iron rod is insufficient to bring them to eternal life.

Others allow these negative influences to grow in their lives until they eventually move from partaking of the tree to mocking from the building. Some of the greatest mockers of the Church enjoyed the fruit of the tree earlier in their lives.

Group Three

Lehi saw other multitudes pressing forward who caught hold of the rod of iron. These people "did press their way forward, continually holding fast to the rod of iron" until they "fell down and partook of the fruit of the tree." (1 Nephi 8:30.) The words "fell down" may be significant, perhaps indicating an act of kneeling in reverence and appreciation for the atonement of the Savior. The previous group partook of the tree but did not fall down. Since nothing more is said of this group, we assume they remained faithful and received all the blessings God has promised the obedient.

This group compares with the people in the parable of the sower who have honest and good hearts. They hear and obey the word of God and endure to the end. These people bring forth the fruits of the Spirit, which allows them in time to become like God.

Group Four

Anyone who is approvingly reading this book can be assured that he is not a member of group four. Lehi saw "other multitudes feeling their way towards that great and spacious building." These people drowned in the depths of the river, entered the large and spacious building, or were lost in other ways as they wandered in "strange roads." (1 Nephi 8:31–32.)

These compare to the people in the parable of the soils who never desired to accept, understand, or live the word of God. They are compared to hard, packed soil that can be found on paths and roads. They harden their hearts so that the word of God can find no place in them. They spend their lives seeking pleasure in sin and wondering why they never feel fulfilled or truly satisfied.

The Importance of the Scriptures

One of the best sources of the word of God is the scriptures. Their importance was emphasized when the Spirit commanded Nephi to slay Laban. When Nephi hesitated, the Spirit explained that "it is better that one man should perish than that a nation should dwindle and perish in unbelief." Nephi then realized that the people "could not keep the commandments of the Lord . . . save they should have the law." (1 Nephi 4:13, 15.)

The Mulekites, who arrived on the American continent from Jerusalem several years after Lehi's group, illustrated this well. They had brought no written records with them; consequently, in time they lost not only any understanding of Jesus and his teachings but even their spoken language, which became so corrupted that the Nephites could not understand them (see Omni 1:17).

Nephi also taught of the importance of the Book of Mormon and other latter-day scripture. He saw in vision that the Bible would come forth from the Jews in purity but would later be altered, evil men taking away from the gospel of Christ "many parts which are plain and most precious." This was done that they might "pervert the right ways of the Lord, . . . blind the eyes and harden the hearts of the children of men." (See 1 Nephi 13:25–29.)

In Nephi's vision, he was told by an angel that "these last records [which would include the Book of Mormon], which thou hast seen among the Gentiles, shall establish the truth of the [Bible] . . . and shall make known the plain and precious things which have been taken away" (1 Nephi 13:40).

We live in a day when the fulness of the gospel—the word of God in its fulness—is available to us. However, unless we read and study the scriptures and the other latter-day sources of inspiration and revelation, we are no better off than the Mulekites, who had no scriptures. The word of God needs to become an integral part of our daily lives.

Conclusion

The dream is simple—the message is clear. The more effort we put into grasping the iron rod, the safer we are when mists of temptation, opposition, and persecution appear in our lives. We grasp the iron rod through study, prayer, obedience, and service. Nephi told us how to stay on the path and receive eternal life:

> Wherefore, my beloved brethren, I know that if ye shall follow the Son, with full purpose of heart, acting no hypocrisy and no deception before God, but with real intent, repenting of your sins, witnessing unto the Father that ye are willing to take upon you the name of Christ, by baptism . . . then shall ye receive the Holy Ghost. . . .
>
> And then are ye in this strait and narrow path which leads to eternal life. . . .
>
> And now, my beloved brethren, after ye have gotten into this strait and narrow path, I would ask if all is done? Behold, I say unto you, Nay; for ye have not come thus far save it were by the word of Christ with unshaken faith in him, relying wholly upon the merits of him who is mighty to save.
>
> Wherefore, ye must press forward with a steadfastness in Christ, having a perfect brightness of hope, and a love of God and of all men. Wherefore, if ye shall press forward, feasting upon the word of Christ, and endure to the end, behold, thus said the Father: Ye shall have eternal life. (2 Nephi 31:13, 18–20.)

Chapter Three

FREE TO ACT
FOR OURSELVES
2 Nephi 2

Agency Is Essential to Progression

In our premortal life we participated in a great council. We heard
Satan present a plan based on force and were intelligent enough to
reject it in favor of our Father's plan. The central ingredient of our
Father's plan was agency, and a war was fought there to protect and
ensure this freedom to choose.

We embraced the plan of agency even though we knew that many
of us might make incorrect choices in mortality and fall short of our
divine potential. The fact that both we and God were willing to take
this risk indicates the monumental importance of agency. In order to
develop the attributes of godliness, freedom of choice is absolutely
necessary. Compulsion and force never lead to spiritual growth. In
fact, most of the time these approaches engender feelings of bitterness, resentment, rebellion, and even hatred.

It is apparent that the prophet Jacob understood the great importance of agency, for he said: "Cheer up your hearts, and remember that
ye are free to act for yourselves—to choose the way of everlasting
death or the way of eternal life" (2 Nephi 10:23).

Satan and much of the world around us would have us believe

otherwise. Almost daily we hear self-negating statements such as "I can't help myself," or "It's not my fault—I was born this way," or "My family brought me up this way and it's too late to change." These and other statements like them are offensive to God and his teachings, for they belittle the fact that we are of celestial parentage and thus inherit the ability to become like our eternal parents. It is a sad thing to see so many people give away their agency and their right to decide what they want to be.

We Are Free to Choose

The reality of our freedom to choose for ourselves was emphasized by Lehi when he taught: "The Messiah cometh in the fulness of time, that he may redeem the children of men from the fall. And because that they are redeemed from the fall they have become free forever, knowing good from evil; to act for themselves and not to be acted upon, save it be by the punishment of the law at the great and last day." Lehi went on to say that we are free to "choose liberty and eternal life, . . . or to choose captivity and death." (2 Nephi 2:26, 27.)

When Lehi taught that because of the Savior's atonement we are free to act for ourselves and not be acted upon, he was including our ability to act, when faced with negative people or situations, as God would have us act, rather than reacting to those around us and allowing them to control our feelings and behavior. To pass that control to others is to give away our agency.

Elder J. Richard Clarke spoke of people who have fallen for the satanic lie that they no longer can control their destiny. One of these was a rapist who, after breaking into a home and raping a young woman for the third time, justified himself by claiming that a hormonal defect had increased his sexual appetite and he could no longer help himself. (See *Brigham Young University 1988–89 Devotional and Fireside Speeches* (Provo, Utah: University Publications, 1989), pp. 98–99.)

Because of alcohol abuse, a man lost his job, his home, and his family. As he loaded up his truck and left the neighborhood, he refused to take any responsibility for his actions. He said that it was all his wife's fault for having an affair with another man.

A woman appeared on a talk show and related that her life had been shattered twenty-three years previously when her brother was murdered. She explained that she had never been able to deal with the murder, had attempted suicide many times, and was still struggling with the pain daily. She claimed that her whole family was torn apart by this murder and that *they* were serving the life sentence. She desired to meet the killer face to face so she could tell him how much she hated him, and she hoped that the memory of what he had done would haunt him for the rest of his life.

These three people blamed others or circumstances for their own weaknesses and unhappiness. Elder F. Burton Howard referred to this attitude when he said:

> Unwillingness to accept the responsibility for and consequences of one's actions is an all too common condition in today's world. Who has not heard of the drunken driver who sues his host for allowing him to get drunk, or of the accident victim who claims damages from the physician who tries to help him? Perpetrators of the most heinous crimes often plead guilty by reason of insanity or claim that they are victims of society's ills. The homeless blame alcohol. Alcoholics blame genetic deficiencies. Abusers and adulterers blame the broken homes of their childhood. And there are enough who agree with them to ensure that no one need feel terribly guilty for long if they don't want to. (*Ensign*, May 1991, p. 12.)

Although all people have received the gift of agency, some have allowed circumstances and others to rob them of their precious gift. The first step in correcting their life course and becoming truly free again through the atonement of Jesus is to begin to take responsibility for their actions.

The Lord has told us that we have the power within us to be agents unto ourselves (see D&C 58:28). Because of the Atonement and with the help of the Spirit, we can position ourselves to better accept God's saving grace. This means that peace, joy, and eternal life are within our grasp, and it is up to us to exercise sufficient faith in Christ to receive these divine gifts.

President George Q. Cannon declared the following message of faith, hope, and comfort:

It is true that some have greater power of resistance than others, but everyone has the power to close his heart against doubt, against darkness, against unbelief, against depression, against anger, against hatred, against jealousy, against malice, against envy. God has given this power unto all of us, and we can gain still greater power by calling upon Him for that which we lack. If it were not so, how could we be condemned for giving way to wrong influences? (*Gospel Truth*, Jerreld L. Newquist, ed. [Salt Lake City: Deseret Book, 1987], pp. 16–17.)

Elder Richard G. Scott also assured us that all of us, even those who have suffered through the devastating effects of abuse, can determine our outcome:

Know that the wicked choice of others cannot completely destroy your agency unless you permit it. Their acts may cause pain, anguish, even physical harm, but they cannot destroy your eternal possibilities in this brief but crucial life on earth. You must understand that you are free to determine to overcome the harmful results of abuse. . . . The laws of your Heavenly Father and the atonement of the Lord have made it possible that you will not be robbed of the opportunities which come to the children of God. (*Ensign*, May 1992, pp. 31–32.)

The Importance of Opposition

Lehi taught that without opposition in all things we could not bring to pass righteousness, holiness, and goodness (see 2 Nephi 2:11). He went on to say, "Man could not act for himself save it should be that he was enticed by the one or the other" (2 Nephi 2:16).

Opposition is one of the necessary ingredients of agency. Without an opportunity to choose between good and evil, we could exercise no choice and therefore no agency. However, opposition plays a much bigger role than just allowing us to choose. It also provides the resistance that we need in order to grow spiritually and develop godly attributes.

We are all aware of the role resistance plays in the growth of physical muscle and strength. Whether that resistance is in the form of weights to lift, stairs to run, or a higher setting on our stationary bicycle, we need resistance in order to develop our physical muscles. Spiritual muscles also require resistance in order to grow.

While in Liberty Jail, Joseph asked the Lord why so many negative things were happening to the Saints and pleaded with Him to intercede in their behalf (see D&C 121:1–6). After listing numerous negative things that Joseph would yet experience, God said, "Know thou, my son, that all these things shall give thee experience, and shall be for thy good. The Son of Man hath descended below them all. Art thou greater than he? . . . Fear not what man can do, for God shall be with you forever and ever." (D&C 122:7–9.)

Through this revelation Joseph learned that opposition was good and needed. He demonstrated his understanding of this principle when he stated:

> I am like a huge, rough stone rolling down from a high mountain; and the only polishing I get is when some corner gets rubbed off by coming in contact with something else, striking with accelerated force against religious bigotry, priestcraft, lawyer-craft, doctor-craft, lying editors, suborned judges and jurors, and the authority of perjured executives, backed by mobs, blasphemers, licentious and corrupt men and women—all hell knocking off a corner here and a corner there. Thus I will become a smooth and polished shaft in the quiver of the Almighty. (*Teachings of the Prophet Joseph Smith*, p. 304.)

Without this adversity, Joseph could not and would not have developed into the great spiritual prophet that he became. Our need for resistance is just as great. We are not born into a world of opposition because God wants to trouble us or punish us for his own whimsical pleasure. Rather, he created this type of world because it is absolutely essential to our becoming like him.

Adversity Does Not Always Lead to Spiritual Growth

One interesting thing about adversity and affliction is that they never leave us untouched and unchanged. For example, we seem to either draw closer to God or further away from him when we face difficulties. Which direction we move depends on our attitude and our faith. Lehi implied to his son Jacob that God would consecrate his afflictions for his gain because Jacob knew the greatness of God (see 2 Nephi 2:2). When circumstances turned sour in Jacob's life, he sought God's help instead of blaming Deity for his problems. Jacob appreciated life's goodness instead of dwelling on its negative side. A sister named Floy taught this same attitude to a young couple who needed it.

One weekend Floy felt a strong urge to visit her grandparents. She reasoned that since it would require driving several hundred miles for only a brief visit, maybe she should visit when there was a holiday—but the feeling persisted.

She arrived late Saturday evening and had a short visit with her grandparents. As she sat in fast and testimony meeting the next morning, she felt the need to stand and bear her testimony. Because it was not her ward, she fought the urge, but soon found herself standing and sharing the story of her experiences with a boy named Charlie.

She met Charlie the first year she taught children with physical handicaps. Charlie's parents had been told when he was born that he would never turn over or lift his head, never walk or talk or do most things that other children do. They were advised to place him in a state institution and go on with their lives.

However, after much prayer the parents decided to keep Charlie and, with the assistance of the Lord, help him develop whatever "potential was stamped upon his soul." After much time, pain, and effort, Charlie learned to speak and walk.

On Floy's first school day, Charlie suggested that they start each class with prayer. Whenever Charlie prayed, "he thanked Heavenly Father for the sunshine on sunny days and for the rain on drizzly days. He was grateful for birds he had seen as he rode to school. And he was always thankful for the progress someone in the class had made the day before. 'Thank you, Heavenly Father, that Nancy learned to tie her shoelaces, and that Mark learned his addings sixes.' Soon all the children wanted a turn at saying the prayer, and the spirit of gratitude, not discouragement, became the standard."

After the meeting closed, a young mother with a baby in her arms stopped Floy and thanked her. She said:

"You may have noticed that on this warm spring day, my baby was kept all bundled up while she was blessed. That is because she has a deformed arm.

"This is the first time I have left our house since she was born," the young mother continued. "I haven't wanted anyone to see her. I didn't even want her blessed in our own ward. I've been worrying about how she may be treated as time goes on. I keep thinking people will stare, and children will make fun of her. I didn't want her to feel that kind of pain."

. . . "Thank you for bearing your testimony today. Through you, the Lord has opened my foolish eyes. I have been hoping for answers to my questions for weeks, but I haven't been ready to listen. I am going to be the best mother the Lord could ever have given her. Together we can meet whatever challenges may come."

The father then lifted back the blanket and the young mother picked up the little baby—uncovered and beautiful. Floy understood at last why God had wanted her to visit her grandparents that weekend. (Floy Daun Mackay, "Beautiful as an Angel," *Ensign,* June 1993, pp. 31–32.)

By focusing on the deformed arm alone, this young couple were restricting their growth as well as the growth of their baby. Once they understood God's goodness in giving them this beautiful baby, her little deformed arm quit being a stumbling block and they began their journey to greater spirituality and personal growth.

Although the story doesn't discuss Charlie's parents, there is no doubt that their dedication to help him grow in spite of his handicaps has brought great patience, understanding, and love into their lives. Because they know the greatness of God and appreciate what they have received, their affliction has truly become a blessing in their lives.

Helping Others Grow Through Agency

It is difficult to see those whom we love make choices that may take them away from God and bring unhappiness into their lives. However, as we try to help, we must remember the importance of agency in spiritual growth. God has told us to specifically avoid compulsion and has emphasized instead that love, meekness, kindness, and the pure knowledge that comes from the Holy Ghost are the tools that lead to righteous change and growth (see D&C 121:37–43). As soon as we begin to manipulate instead of encourage, the Lord's Spirit withdraws from us and we lose the guidance that we desperately need. Elder Marion D. Hanks emphasized this important principle when he said:

> Instruction and rules and training and discipline are essential, of course. From our Father's example of godly love and patience, we should be motivated to stretch to any lengths to teach, to persuade, to encourage, to help.
>
> But in matters of conscience and faith, if we truly love we will never seek to impose our will and deprive others of their agency. That is, after all, Satan's way. (*Ensign,* November 1983, p. 22.)

We Are Never Alone

All of us face tragedy, death, sickness, and many other disasters that can bring heartache into our lives. The sad thing is that many continue to feel anguish and sorrow long after they need to. Though the original pain may have been caused by events beyond their control, the continued pain comes through their own actions and attitudes. They allow hate, bitterness, and loneliness to canker their souls and destroy their lives. They do not properly exercise the great gift of agency that allows us, with God's help, to control not only our actions but also our desires and feelings. Jesus offered peace and rest from the turmoil and disasters of the world when he said: "Come unto me, all ye that labour and are heavy laden, and I will give you rest. Take my yoke upon you, and learn of me; for I am meek and lowly in heart: and ye shall find rest unto your souls." (Matthew 11:28–29.)

Through the atonement and grace of Jesus Christ, which is always available to those who exercise faith in him, we can become truly free. Because of Jesus, we can "act for ourselves" and keep circumstances and other people from dictating how we feel and how we act. Agency not only allows us to grow and become like God, it also allows us to enjoy this life and have control over our feelings and actions. Few gospel principles are as important as the absolutely indispensable opportunity we have to choose for ourselves.

Chapter Four

AN INFINITE
ATONEMENT
2 Nephi 9

We Are Saved by Grace

In an *Ensign* article, Bruce C. Hafen quoted from a 1980 *Newsweek* report as follows: "Unlike orthodox Christians, Mormons believe that men are born free of sin and earn their way to godhood by the proper exercise of free will, rather than through the grace of Jesus Christ. Thus Jesus' suffering and death in the Mormon view . . . do not atone for the sins of others." (*Newsweek*, 1 September 1980, p. 68, as quoted in *Ensign*, April 1990, p. 7.) Apparently *Newsweek* based their statement on interviews with members of the Church who were asked what they actually believed.

This article is troubling because, as Brother Hafen points out, the atoning role of Christ in the process of salvation is *the* core doctrine of the Church. That some members of the Church do not realize their complete dependance on Christ not only shows a limited understanding of the gospel but also suggests that they are not partaking of the enabling power and help that Christ offers. Quite seriously, their eternal future may be in jeopardy.

Since becoming familiar with this survey, I have asked numerous groups of adults whether we are saved by grace, and the answer is always no. They usually base their answer on 2 Nephi 25:23, which states, "We know that it is by grace that we are saved, after all we can do." Because of the widespread erroneous teaching that we will be saved by grace no matter what we do, members of the Church often overreact and wrongly claim that we cannot be saved by grace. Nephi did not say that we are saved *by* "all we can do," for there is no way any of us can do enough good works to save ourselves. Clearly we are saved by grace. This critical concept was recently illustrated in a story told by Elder Ronald E. Poelman of the Seventy:

> Recently I was in private conversation with one who, having committed a serious transgression, had also made intense effort to repent and receive forgiveness from those personally offended, from the Church, and from the Lord. When I asked, "Do you feel forgiven by your Heavenly Father?" he answered hesitantly with an affirmative but qualified response. "How do we obtain divine forgiveness?" I asked.
>
> He spoke of how he had forsaken his transgressive behavior of the past, confessed to proper priesthood authorities, and attempted to make restitution to those offended. He further described his efforts to live according to gospel principles and Church standards.
>
> The Savior and his atoning sacrifice were not mentioned. The underlying assumption seemed to be that divine forgiveness is obtained through those steps of repentance limited to changing one's behavior. Despite the brother's earnest efforts to repent, he appeared to be burdened still by remorse and regret and to feel that he must continue to pay for his sins.
>
> . . . The fact is we cannot save ourselves. (*Ensign*, November 1993, p. 84.)

Nephi wrote of the central importance the Savior had in the lives of his people: "And we talk of Christ, we rejoice in Christ, we preach of Christ, we prophesy of Christ, and we write according to our prophecies, that our children may know to what source they may look for a remission of their sins" (2 Nephi 25:26).

Do we talk of Christ, rejoice in Christ, and preach of Christ? In our private and public prayers do we mention gratitude for the atonement of Christ? Are the decisions we make centered around the Savior and his teachings? The following statement is taken from a letter that Elder Dallin H. Oaks once received from a member of the Church living in the United States: "I sat and listened to seventeen testimonies and never heard Jesus mentioned or referred to in any way. . . . The following Sunday, I again attended church. I sat through a priesthood lesson, a Gospel Doctrine lesson, and seven sacrament meeting speakers and never once heard the name of Jesus or any reference to him." (*Ensign,* November 1990, p. 30.)

After I read of these incidents, I made the decision to jot down, during a recent testimony meeting I attended what subjects were mentioned. People expressed gratitude for neighbors, friends, the gospel, the Church, the prophet, family members, the bishopric, teachers, blessings they had received, and answers to their prayers. The Savior's name was never mentioned except when people closed their remarks in his name, nor did any refer to the Atonement, repentance, or forgiveness. The seriousness of these oversights is not that Jesus was not mentioned but that he was apparently not thought of. When we rejoice in his atonement and love him for what he has done and is doing for us, our feelings are reflected in everything that we do and say.

As I contemplated this fast and testimony meeting, this scripture came to mind: "In nothing doth man offend God . . . save those who confess not his hand in all things" (D&C 59:21). This experience has caused me to examine my own feelings concerning the Savior and his atonement and to refocus my gratitude on his wonderful grace. In the LDS Bible Dictionary *grace* is defined as follows:

> The main idea of the word is *divine means of help or strength*, given through the bounteous mercy and love of Jesus Christ. . . .
> . . . This grace is an *enabling power* that allows men and women to lay hold on eternal life and exaltation after they have expended their own best efforts.
> Divine grace is needed by every soul in consequence of the fall of Adam and also because of man's weaknesses and shortcomings. (P. 697; emphasis added.)

This divine help that we call grace comes to us in at least four different ways. Some blessings come to us no matter what we do. Other blessings become available to us as we live the gospel, but it is important to realize that none of these blessings is really earned. The small portion we contribute is miniscule compared to the blessings we receive in return.

The rest of this chapter focuses on the various blessings of the Atonement.

The Gift of the Resurrection

President Thomas S. Monson said: "We laugh, we cry, we work, we play, we love, we live. And then we die. And dead we would remain but for one man and his mission, even Jesus of Nazareth." (*Ensign,* April 1990, p. 5.) Through his own resurrection Jesus broke the bands of death, and he now gives this gift freely to every human being. Alma explained this universal resurrection: "The spirit and the body shall be reunited again in its perfect form. . . . Now, this restoration shall come to all, both old and young, both bond and free, both male and female, both the wicked and the righteous; and even there shall not so much as a hair of their heads be lost; but every thing shall be restored to its perfect frame." (Alma 11:43–44.)

It is of great importance to have the doctrine of the resurrection taught with clarity, for much of the Christian world believes that resurrection consists solely of the spirit rising to heaven. In our quest for godhood, gaining a physical body again is absolutely essential, for "spirit and element, inseparably connected" are necessary in order to receive a "fulness of joy" (D&C 93:33).

Our appreciation for the wonderful, freely given gift of resurrection deepens when we realize the alternative. Jacob emphasized this when he stated:

> O the wisdom of God, his mercy and grace! For behold, if the flesh should rise no more our spirits must become subject to that angel who fell from before the presence of the Eternal God, and became the devil, to rise no more.
>
> And our spirits must have become like unto him, and we become devils, angels to a devil, to be shut out from the presence of our God,

and to remain with the father of lies, in misery, like unto himself. . . .

O how great the goodness of our God, who prepareth a way for our escape from the grasp of this awful monster. (2 Nephi 9:8–10.)

The Gift of Forgiveness

The scriptures teach us that a punishment is attached to every broken law. This punishment includes "remorse of conscience" (see Alma 42:18). This punishment was referred to by King Benjamin when he said: "Therefore if that man repenteth not, and remaineth and dieth an enemy to God, the demands of divine justice do awaken his immortal soul to a lively sense of his own guilt, which doth cause him to shrink from the presence of the Lord, and doth fill his breast with guilt, and pain, and anguish, which is like an unquenchable fire" (Mosiah 2:38).

The good news for us is that Jesus was willing to take this pain upon himself so that those who truly repent can avoid this suffering and be cleansed of their sins. Jesus clearly described this incredible blessing in section 19 of the Doctrine and Covenants: "For behold, I, God [Jesus], have suffered these things for all, that they might not suffer if they would repent; but if they would not repent they must *suffer even as I*; which suffering caused myself, even God, . . . to tremble because of pain, and to bleed at every pore, and to suffer both body and spirit" (D&C 19:16–18).

Elder Neal A. Maxwell testified of this important concept in this succinct statement: "We will end up either choosing Christ's manner of living or His manner of suffering!" (*Ensign,* May 1987, p. 72.) President Marion G. Romney helped us better understand the extent of this suffering when he stated: "No man, nor set of men, nor all men put together, ever suffered what the Redeemer suffered in the Garden" (*Improvement Era*, December 1953, p. 942).

Sometimes we may feel that we earn the gift of forgiveness through repentance, but we do not—indeed, we cannot. Repentance may qualify us to receive forgiveness, but there is no way that this gift can be earned. Jesus, who lived a sinless life and therefore did not have to suffer for sin, willingly volunteered to suffer for our sins because of his great love for us. It is not possible to repay this debt, but through repentance and obedience we can accept his wonderful gift and show the Savior we appreciate eternally what he has done for us.

The Gift of Enabling Power

Not only will the Savior forgive us as we repent, but also he will give us the *power* to overcome our sins and keep his commandments. We all have weaknesses that, no matter how hard we try, we cannot overcome on our own. When we do our best to overcome these problems, the Lord will bless us with the extra strength that we need to successfully live the gospel. Nephi testified that "the Lord giveth no commandments unto the children of men, save he shall prepare a way for them that they may accomplish the thing which he commandeth them" (1 Nephi 3:7). The Savior promised us that he would help us repent and even make our weaknesses become strengths: "My grace is sufficient for all men that humble themselves before me; for if they humble themselves before me, and have faith in me, then will I make weak things become strong unto them" (Ether 12:27).

Some people mistakenly feel that they can overcome their sins and become perfect through their own efforts, as if hard work and a positive attitude alone will save their souls. When they run up against commandments they can't keep and character traits they can't develop, many become discouraged and quit trying. The good news is that Jesus will help us become like him. This help becomes available to us as we become his disciples and exercise faith in him by doing his will:

> Through the Holy Ghost, the Atonement makes possible certain spiritual endowments that actually purify our nature and enable us to live a more "eternal" or Godlike life. . . . Then we will exhibit divine character not just because we think we should, but because that is the way we are.
>
> The gift of *charity* illustrates this process. . . . This love . . . is not developed entirely by our own power, even though our faithfulness is a necessary qualification to receive it. Rather, charity is *bestowed* upon the "true followers" of Christ (see Moroni 7:48). Its source, like all other

blessings of the Atonement, is the grace of God. (Bruce C. Hafen, *Ensign*, April 1990, p. 12.)

In the last chapter of the Book of Mormon, Moroni shares with us what we must do to receive Jesus' help in gaining perfection: "Yea, come unto Christ, and be perfected in him, and deny yourselves of all ungodliness; and if ye shall deny yourselves of all ungodliness, and love God with all your might, mind and strength, then is his grace sufficient for you, that by his grace ye may be perfect in Christ" (Moroni 10:32).

An inmate gave the following testimony during a religious service in a state prison. Notice how the Lord helped him repent and prepare himself for baptism into the kingdom of God.

> Over the past month the Lord has given me so many blessings. He's changed my heart. He's taken away the anger, hatred, and fear. He's replaced these with love and hope. He's also taken away my foul mouth and my desire for tobacco. He's helping me to overcome many fleshly weaknesses. . . .
>
> I truly want to be baptized . . . a member of The Church of Jesus Christ of Latter-day Saints. I believe it is His Church and know my lifelong search is over. (Reported by Elder J. Richard Clarke, *Ensign*, May 1993, p. 10.)

The Gift of Peace

God has never promised us an easy life, but he does not leave us on our own. Sometimes he heals us or removes an affliction. On other occasions he blesses us with power to endure or even overcome our problems. But the Lord has promised throughout the scriptures one blessing that we can have in all situations in this life—peace. Repeatedly the Savior promises us peace in this life and eternal life in the world to come. There is perhaps no greater gift in this life than to have God's peace during times of turmoil. Whether we experience the death of a loved one, weather-related disaster, loss of employment, serious sickness, or any of numerous other problems, inner peace can be ours through God's loving grace.

A *Church News* editorial discussed this peace that Jesus offers: "We know the peace Jesus offers as tranquility of the soul, or inner peace. It is mighty and powerful. It is indestructible and immune to the actions of others. It can endure *all* calamity, *every* disaster, *all* manner of turmoil. It enables individuals to rise above whatever tumult surrounds them. (December 19, 1992.)

The scriptures are filled with references to this peace. Jacob wrote that the word of God heals the wounded soul (see Jacob 2:8). Nephi testified that Jesus knows those who follow him, and he feeds them and gives them pasture (see 1 Nephi 22:25). Alma taught that Jesus suffered afflictions, temptations, and infirmities of every kind so he would know how to succor us (see Alma 7:11–12). The second verse of the well-loved hymn "I Know That My Redeemer Lives" refers to this wonderful part of the Atonement:

> He lives to grant me rich supply.
> He lives to guide me with his eye.
> He lives to comfort me when faint.
> He lives to hear my soul's complaint.
> He lives to silence all my fears.
> He lives to wipe away my tears.
> He lives to calm my troubled heart.
> He lives all blessings to impart.
>
> (*Hymns*, no. 136.)

Three Ways the Savior's Atonement Is Infinite

1. *Jesus is an infinite being.* Jesus is unlike any other man born on the earth, in that he had a mortal mother (Mary) and an immortal father (Heavenly Father). From his mother he inherited the power to die; from his Father he inherited power over death—the power to live forever.

Amulek referred to Jesus' special nature in this way: "For it is expedient that there should be a great and last sacrifice; yea, not a sacrifice of man, neither of beast, neither of any manner of fowl; for it shall not be a human sacrifice; but it must be an infinite and eternal sacrifice. . . . That great and last sacrifice will be the Son of God, yea, infinite and eternal." (Alma 34:10, 14.)

Although we do not understand how, Jesus was able to suffer for our sins, our sufferings, even our sicknesses, and break the bands of death because of his eternal nature. Jesus was not only sinless but was also the Son of God and as such possessed the powers of God.

2. *The Atonement is infinite because it includes all of the worlds that Jesus has created.* Joseph Smith's vision of the three degrees of glory revealed that "through him, and of him, the worlds are and were created, and the inhabitants thereof are begotten sons and daughters unto God" (D&C 76:24). Joseph later wrote a poetic rendering of this marvelous vision, which adds to our understanding of the Atonement. The following excerpt from his poem correlates with the above passage of scripture:

> And I heard a great voice, bearing record from heav'n,
> "He's the Saviour, and Only begotten of God;
> By him, of him, and through him, the worlds were all made,
> Even all that careen in the heavens so broad,
> Whose inhabitants, too, from the first to the last,
> Are sav'd by the very same Savior of ours;"
>
> (*Times and Seasons* 4:82–83.)

3. *The Atonement is infinite because it encompasses the past, the present, and the future.* In section 20 of the Doctrine and Covenants we read "that as many as would believe and be baptized in his holy name, and endure in faith to the end, should be saved—not only those who believed after he came in the meridian of time, in the flesh, but all those from the beginning, even as many as were before he came, who believed in the words of the holy prophets, . . . should have eternal life" (D&C 20:25–26).

Just as we look back in history to study his life, sacrifice, and atonement, those who lived before the birth of Christ were encouraged to "look forward unto the Messiah, and believe in him to come as though he already was" (Jarom 1:11).

Conclusion

Alan Czenkusch is the leader of the Whistepig Climbing School of Del Norte, Colorado. He once fell from a high precipice, yanking out three mechanical supports and pulling his climbing companion off a ledge. He was stopped upside down just ten feet from the ground when his spread-eagled companion halted his fall with the strength of his outstretched arms.

"Don saved my life," says Czenkusch. "How do you respond to a guy like that? Give him a used climbing rope for a Christmas present? No, you remember him. You always remember him." (Eric G. Anderson, "The Vertical Wilderness," *Private Practice,* November 1979, p. 21.)

That is what we can do, should do, for the Savior. We can remember him. We can remember his loving kindness and his priesthood power. We can remember what he has done for us and show our appreciation to him by following his commandments and becoming more like him. We can show our love for him by serving others and helping those around us come to love and appreciate him more. We can remember him by devoting our lives to our Father in Heaven and the building up of his kingdom here on the earth. We can remember him by striving to become as he is. We can make him and his teachings the central focus of our lives. We can remember him in all that we do. We can always remember him.

Chapter Five

THE CUNNING AND CRAFTINESS OF SATAN
2 Nephi 28

Jesus Offers Exaltation to Everyone

We are all children of God; he plays no favorites. He offers exaltation to everyone and does everything he can do to make this offer fruitful. We each decide whether we will accept his love and generosity by how we react to his plan. Nephi stressed the unlimited scope of the Savior's love when he wrote:

> He doeth not anything save it be for the benefit of the world; for he loveth the world, even that he layeth down his own life that he may draw all men unto him. Wherefore, he commandeth none that they shall not partake of his salvation.
>
> Behold, doth he cry unto any, saying: Depart from me? Behold, I say unto you, Nay; but he saith: Come unto me all ye ends of the earth. . . .
>
> Behold, hath the Lord commanded any that they should not partake of his goodness? Behold I say unto you, Nay; but all men are privileged the one like unto the other, and none are forbidden. (2 Nephi 26:24–25, 28.)

When our Heavenly Father sent us down to this earth to work out our salvation, he did not leave us alone. He realized that we could not become like him without his help. As discussed in the previous chapter, the most important help he gives us comes through the atoning sacrifice of our Savior. Without the Atonement, all of us would be lost. But he has given us other help as well.

He has preserved powerful writings of spiritual men through the centuries. As we read their teachings and testimonies, our hearts fill with understanding, inspiration, and power. Further, we have been given living prophets that address the problems we face today. Most important, he has invited us to communicate directly with him. What a blessing—to speak directly to our Father in Heaven and, through the Holy Ghost, receive the comfort, direction, and inspiration that we so desperately need. By allowing us to communicate with him, our Father is telling us that each of his children is important to him.

A teenage girl (let's call her Jan) demonstrated the great importance of realizing we are personally loved by our Father in Heaven. She attended a seminary class for four days and then ran away from home. Her parents were distressed; no one knew where she was, and days went by with no word from her.

About two o'clock one morning, her seminary teacher's phone rang and a long-distance operator asked if he would accept a collect call. He agreed, and the next voice that he heard was Jan's. She thanked her teacher for taking the call and asked him if she could talk to him for a minute. When he agreed, she explained that during one of the four days she had been in his class, he had said that no matter what a person did, right or wrong, Heavenly Father still loved that person. Now she wanted to know whether he really knew that was true. When he assured her that it was, she spent twenty minutes describing what had happened since she had run away. She then returned home and began to change her life for the better.

The teacher did not even remember making the statement in class, but she did, and she needed the assurance that God loved her in order to start her way back to the Lord. (CES Teleconference Packet, 6–24–89, p. 34.)

Many Reject the Love Jesus Offers

It is a sad reality that many reject the wonderful love and blessings God offers them. After watching hundreds of thousands of people die by the sword, Mormon lamented:

> And my soul was rent with anguish, because of the slain of my people, and I cried:
>
> O ye fair ones, how could ye have departed from the ways of the Lord! O ye fair ones, how could ye have rejected that Jesus, *who stood with open arms to receive you!*
>
> Behold, if ye had not done this, ye would not have fallen. But behold, ye are fallen, and I mourn your loss.
>
> O ye fair sons and daughters, ye fathers and mothers, ye husbands and wives, ye fair ones, how is it that ye could have fallen!
>
> But behold, ye are gone, and my sorrows cannot bring your return. (Mormon 6:16–20, emphasis added.)

It is difficult to read this passage without feeling Mormon's great love for his people. He ached for their suffering and death that came because they rejected the Savior and his teachings. His anguish gives us but a glimpse of how our Father in Heaven must feel when we refuse the love he offers us.

Many people reject the gospel in their misguided quest for happiness. Not realizing the true source of happiness, they spend their time seeking pleasure and experimenting with the quick fix. This mind-set was never more obvious than in a newspaper I read that had thirty-four personal ads by psychics. It is apparent that these people make their living by promising instant happiness.

All of the ads had something in common. They promised almost instant happiness, success, wealth, love, or any other desire. Such ads are just one of a multitude of temptations that Satan employs to cloud our focus and derail our progression. He uses cunning and craftiness to make things seem different than they really are. If we are not careful, he gets us to spend our time and money "for that which cannot satisfy" (2 Nephi 9:51).

The Symptoms of Spiritual Illness

Because of Satan's ability to package sin so attractively, the world is filled with people who are spiritually ill. To diagnose and treat physical illness, we must learn to recognize the symptoms. So it is with spiritual illness. The first step in healing spiritual illness is to recognize there is a problem and begin to act accordingly. In 2 Nephi 28, Nephi describes ten spiritual ills that will exist in the latter days. As we discuss these problems, it will be helpful for each of us to evaluate our own life and make sure that we are free of these Satan-inspired attitudes.

1. *Churches that claim to be true but are filled with contention* (see verses 3–4). At first glance this problem may not seem applicable to us, but the word *contention* makes it applicable. We claim to be members of the true church. Do we feel contention in our hearts? Do we have contentious feelings against Church leaders, ward members, or other people we come into contact with? Contention comes directly from the devil and is an important symptom of a lack of the Spirit. Unity and oneness are signs of the Lord's people.

2. *"They shall teach with their learning, and deny the Holy Ghost"* (verse 4). Some deny the Holy Ghost by rejecting the restored gospel. But those who have accepted the gospel often deny the Holy Ghost simply by doing little to seek his guidance. As we rear our children, teach lessons, serve in the Church, and associate with others daily, do we seek the influence of the Holy Ghost or do we rely on our own learning? No attitude is more destructive than to go through life feeling that we do not need the Lord's assistance.

3. *"And they deny the power of God"* (verses 5–6). Many feel that God is no longer a God of miracles and therefore reject the prophets whom God has called in our time. Others accept the fact that God's power is on the earth but become selective in what they accept from the prophets. However, the most common way in which Latter-day Saints reject God's power is by failing to develop the faith and works necessary to enjoy the gifts of the Spirit. These Saints believe that God has great power and that he answers prayers. They just don't believe he will answer *their* prayers or give *them* the power they need. They turn down Church callings or fail to do their home or visiting teaching because they feel inadequate; they fail to overcome personal weaknesses because they don't have enough willpower and in many

other ways refuse to use God's power in their lives. They believe *in* God, but they don't believe God; that is, they don't believe him when he promises that he will empower them to accomplish anything that he asks them to do (see 1 Nephi 3:7). They deny, through the way they live, the power of God.

4. *Many shall teach that some sin and wickedness is okay* (see verses 7–9). Nephi pointed out that many will feel justified in "committing a little sin," in lying a little, and in taking advantage of their neighbor: for "if it so be that we are guilty, God will beat us with a few stripes, and at last we shall be saved in the kingdom of God." These people seek to hide their activities from God by doing their works in the dark (as if God couldn't see them). Nephi called these ideas "false and vain and foolish doctrines."

Notice the emphasis that Satan places on the word *little*, suggesting that some sins will not hurt us—as long as they are not "big sins." Not only is this perception false, but the fact is that small sins nearly always lead to bigger ones.

President Gordon B. Hinckley once related an experience of a seemingly small sin that led to great ones. He told of a man who held highly responsible positions in both the Church and the community and was sealed to a wonderful wife and family. His trouble began when he picked up a pornographic magazine to read on a plane. He found the magazine so exciting that he later purchased more of them. His desire to be stimulated in this way increased, and he soon started to seek out inappropriate movies. Realizing that his wife would have nothing to do with this type of activity, he found reasons to go to other cities where he could more easily indulge his desires without fear of getting found out by his wife or others.

He soon began to find excuses to stay late at his office and asked his secretary to stay with him. It wasn't long until he and his secretary were involved in immoral behavior, and he ended up being excommunicated from the Church.

The man had endured four years of heartache when President Hinckley met with him to see if he was worthy to have his Church blessings restored. With tears rolling down his cheeks, the man cursed the day that he had read that first magazine. "He spoke of his love for the wife who had forgiven him and remained true to him. He spoke of his love for his children, who had been shamed and embarrassed by his actions. He told of the hell through which he had walked for some four years from the time of his excommunication." (*Ensign,* May 1983, pp. 51–52.)

All of this could have been avoided had the man not fallen for the satanic lie that looking at a pornographic magazine is not really that big of a sin. The truth is that all sin—big or small—restricts the help we receive from God and increases Satan's influence—even power—over us.

5. *Because of pride they have become corrupt* (see verses 10–12). It is interesting that in Lehi's vision of the tree of life, the only sin depicted was pride. Latter-day prophets have indicated that pride is the source of nearly every sin that we commit. Pride is the great stumbling-block to personal revelation and spiritual growth, for humility (the opposite of pride) is absolutely essential in communication with God. You will probably notice that most of the sins included in this list have something to do with pride.

6. *"They rob the poor because of their fine clothing"* (verse 13). James taught us that a major part of true religion is "to visit the fatherless and widows in their affliction" (James 1:27). In our day God declared, "And remember in all things the poor and the needy, the sick and the afflicted, for he that doeth not these things, the same is not my disciple" (D&C 52:40).

Could Nephi's statement that "they rob the poor because of their fine clothing," mean in today's context that maybe we spend too much money on luxuries, which leaves us with no money to help the needy? When we compare our circumstances in North America to much of the world, we find that most of what we own are luxuries. This problem of robbing the poor was discussed in a multi-area conference involving several stakes that were situated in affluent areas; yet despite the comparative wealth of these stakes, the fast offering paid each year did not meet the needs of the poor within the stakes' boundaries, let alone the thousands of Church members in nonaffluent countries that desperately need our help.

Remember that we have been asked to search our hearts and contribute a *generous* fast offering in addition to our collective and individual responsibility to help those less fortunate than ourselves in a variety of ways.

7. *"They have all gone astray save it be a few"* (verse 14). Satan's persuasions are so effective that often only a relatively few, respond to the Spirit and strive to keep God's commandments. Not only are there numerous non-Christian religions but hundreds of Christian churches "teach for doctrines the commandments of men, having a form of godliness, but they deny the power thereof" (JS—H 1:19). These doctrines include such concepts as God's having no body, parts, or passions; being a personage of spirit only; and that revelation has ceased. They teach that children are born sinful and, if not baptized before death, will never be able to live with God. Some claim that homosexuality and abortion are not sins and vote on what their policies and doctrines will be. No wonder the Savior told Joseph Smith that their "creeds were an abomination in his sight" (JS—H 1:19).

8. *Many humble followers of Christ are led away; they err; and people rage against that which is good* (see verses 14, 20). Satan is so successful that in many matters much of the world teaches things that are wrong. They present such falsehoods so logically that, without the guidance of the Spirit and the prophets, we can be easily led astray. There are those who denounce good things as evil, and promote evil things as good. For example, some say that to be against the homosexual movement is to show prejudice and narrow-mindedness; to be against abortion is to be anti-woman and to deprive women of their rights; and to seek to be a homemaker instead of a career woman is to demonstrate laziness or lack of brains and talent.

In contrast, humble lovers of eternal truth teach that the keys to walking the path that leads to eternal life—in a world that is accelerating in the opposite direction—are personal and family prayer, personal and family scripture study, family home evening, listening to and following the living prophets, and doing our very best to live the gospel. If we do not pay close attention to the word of God, Satan's mists may soon cause us to lose our way.

9. *Satan will pacify them and "lull them away into carnal*

security" (see verse 21). Nephi prophesied that many active Church members will say, "All is well in Zion; yea, Zion prospereth, all is well—and thus the devil . . . leadeth them carefully down to hell" (verse 21). The word *carefully* suggests that slowly but surely Satan gains increasing control over people without their being aware of their straying.

Those Saints who are sincerely striving to become more like God never feel that "all is well," for they perceive the great gap that exists between where they are and what they need to become. However, recognizing this gap does not bring discouragement, for they know that as they do their best God will give them the power to become like him.

10. *"Others he flattereth away, and telleth them there is [no devil and] no hell"* (verses 22–23). If we accept that there is no devil and no hell, then the logical extension is that there is no sin. We have only to look around us to see how many people have fallen for this destructive lie.

Nephi stated that Satan "whispereth in their ears, until he grasps them with his awful chains." The word *whispereth* reveals the sneaky and cunning nature of Satan's temptations. By nudging us in a quiet way to commit some small indiscretion or to think some almost trivial half-truth, he slowly and carefully guides us along until he has us completely in his grasp.

The Spirit Will Not Always Strive with Man

Nephi taught that "the Spirit of the Lord will not always strive with man. And when the Spirit ceaseth to strive with man then cometh speedy destruction." (2 Nephi 26:11.) In our quest for eternal life, perhaps the single most important thing we can have is the companionship and help of the Holy Ghost. To lose his guidance and power is spiritually fatal. We do not have to be perfect in order to enjoy the companionship of the Holy Ghost, but we do have to be trying to live the gospel and sincerely desire to do what God wants us to do.

It is vital to remember that God loves us and wants us to succeed. God's plan works. Because of the help that he is willing to give us, we can each enjoy eternal life if we but do our best. President Ezra Taft Benson made each of us an encouraging promise when he said, "If we give our all, we will get his all from the greatest of all" (*Ensign,* July 1975, p. 63).

Chapter Six

THE STRAIT AND NARROW PATH
2 Nephi 31

Introduction

On one occasion our family drove from Salt Lake City, Utah, to Boston, Massachusetts, which is probably a distance of around two thousand miles. Without a road map the trip would have been long and miserable, if not impossible. In fact we would not have even considered the trip without a good up-to-date road map.

In a sense we can compare our family trip to Boston with our situation here on earth. Our planned destination is the celestial kingdom, but we have hundreds of invitations to do evil every day. If we accept these invitations, we find ourselves on roads that will never—and can never—take us where we want to go. That is why God has given us prophets, both past and present, to help us find and stay on the path.

Nephi explained how to get on this path when he said, "The gate by which ye should enter is repentance and baptism by water; and then cometh a remission of your sins by fire and by the Holy Ghost. And then are ye in this strait and narrow path which leads to eternal life." (2 Nephi 31:17–18.) This scripture underscores the essential nature of both repentance and baptism, which will be briefly discussed.

Turning the Heart Toward God

Even though the principles governing repentance are simple, many misunderstand what repentance is and how to take advantage of it. One common definition of repentance is "to stop doing something wrong and start doing something right." Although changing behavior is included in true repentance, this statement is a long way from completely explaining what sincere repentance really is. President Ezra Taft Benson discussed this idea of repentance when he stated:

> Many men and women in the world demonstrate great willpower and self-discipline in overcoming bad habits and the weaknesses of the flesh. Yet at the same time they give no thought to the Master, sometimes even openly rejecting Him. Such changes of behavior, even if in a positive direction, do not constitute true repentance.
>
> Faith in the Lord Jesus Christ is the foundation upon which sincere and meaningful repentance must be built. (*Ensign*, October 1989, p. 2.)

People may stop smoking, decide to spend more time with their families, or resolve to forgive someone. Although these changes in their lives will bring them more happiness, they do not guarantee that true repentance has taken place. Repentance has much to do with the heart and is effected on a much broader scale than just changing one problem area of our lives. The LDS Bible Dictionary indicates that the Greek word that is translated as *repentance* in the scriptures "denotes a change of mind, i.e., a fresh view about God, about oneself, and about the world. Since we are born into conditions of mortality, repentance comes to mean a turning of the heart and will to God, and a renunciation of sin."

Repentance must center in and around the Savior and his atonement. Without him and his atoning sacrifice, there would be neither repentance nor forgiveness.

A Total Commitment to God and His Way of Life

Sometimes we feel that we understand some gospel principle so well that we fail to continue to study and learn about that particular principle. It may be taught so often or seem so simple that when we have to give a lesson or a talk on the subject we just refer to the information we have used in the past. This is a dangerous trap to fall into, for our lack of study and prayer may keep us from progressing in understanding and applying the gospel.

A Latter-day Saint named Lance fell into this very trap regarding the principle of repentance. He taught it the same way each year and never did much additional study or research until he ran across the following scripture: "For whosoever shall keep the whole law, and yet offend in one point, he is guilty of all. For he that said, Do not commit adultery, said also, Do not kill. Now if thou commit no adultery, yet if thou kill, thou art become a transgressor of the law." (James 2:10–11.)

As Lance read this scripture over and over again, he kept asking himself, "How can this be? How can I be guilty of breaking all of the laws if I only break one of them?" This didn't fit into his understanding of repentance at all. After several hours of researching the scriptures and the words of the prophets, he came to understand this scripture and the whole principle of repentance much better. He learned that the key to understanding this scripture is to know what law we need to keep in order not to be offenders. During the last week of his mortal ministry, Jesus explained:

> Thou shalt love the Lord thy God with all thy heart, and with all thy soul, and with all thy mind.
>
> This is the first and great commandment.
>
> And the second is like unto it, Thou shalt love thy neighbour as thyself.
>
> On these two commandments hang all the law and the prophets. (Matthew 22:37–40.)

The great law that we need to keep is to love God with all our hearts, souls, and minds, and then to love our neighbors as ourselves. Every other commandment that God has given us simply tells us how to love God and our fellowmen. If we love God we will attend church, treat others with compassion, and strive to do everything else God wants us to do. Jesus made this plain when he said, "If ye love me, keep my commandments. . . . He that hath my commandments, and keepeth them, he it is that loveth me." (John 14:15, 21.)

Repentance, then, is a process of turning our attitudes, desires, and actions toward God. When our hearts are pure and we are willing to do whatever God wants us to do, we become repentant and, therefore, are in a position to be forgiven. President Spencer W. Kimball taught:

> Repentance must involve an all-out, total surrender to the program of the Lord. That transgressor is not fully repentant who neglects his tithing, misses his meetings, breaks the Sabbath, fails in his family prayers, does not sustain the authorities of the Church, breaks the Word of Wisdom, does not love the Lord nor his fellowmen. A reforming adulterer who drinks or curses is not repentant. The repenting burglar who has sex play is not ready for forgiveness. God cannot forgive unless the transgressor shows a true repentance which spreads to all areas of his life. (*The Miracle of Forgiveness* [Salt Lake City: Bookcraft, 1969], p. 203.)

A Mighty Change in Our Hearts

The Nephite people at the time of King Benjamin described a significant change in their very souls as they sought and obtained forgiveness: "Because of the Spirit of the Lord Omnipotent, which has wrought a mighty change in us, or in our hearts, . . . we have no more disposition to do evil, but to do good continually" (Mosiah 5:2). The scriptures refer to this "mighty change" as being born again. Wisely did the Nephite people realize that this change came through the cleansing and transforming power of the Holy Ghost.

King Benjamin indicated that this change of heart comes not only through the Holy Ghost but also through the atonement of Jesus:

> For the natural man is an enemy to God, and has been from the fall of Adam, and will be, forever and ever, unless he yields to the enticings of the Holy Spirit, and putteth off the natural man and becometh a saint through the atonement of Christ the Lord, and becometh as a child, submissive, meek, humble, patient, full of love, willing to submit to all

things which the Lord seeth fit to inflict upon him, even as a child doth submit to his father (Mosiah 3:19).

Perfection Not Required for Repentance

Repentance requires a sincere, 100 percent effort, accompanied by the realization that God will help us grow toward perfection as we do our very best. Elder Bruce R. McConkie explained the relationship between repentance, effort, and perfection in this way:

> We don't need to get a complex or get a feeling that you have to be perfect to be saved. You don't. . . . What you have to do is get on the straight and narrow path—thus charting a course leading to eternal life—and then, being on that path, pass out of this life in full fellowship. I'm not saying that you don't have to keep the commandments. I'm saying you don't have to be perfect to be saved. . . . What you have to do is stay in the mainstream of the Church and live as upright and decent people live in the Church—keeping the commandments, paying your tithing, serving in the organizations of the Church, loving the Lord, staying on the straight and narrow path. (Fireside, Salt Lake Institute, University of Utah, January 10, 1982, p. 9.)

A Process, Not an Event

Sometimes we read about great men whose lives seemed to change in a matter of hours or days, men such as Paul and Alma the Younger. If we are not careful we might begin to think that this is the norm for repentance and spiritual growth. Actually, such dramatic experiences are the exception rather than the rule. For most of us, the process of repentance is much more imperceptible. Day by day we strive to keep the commandments, serve others, and fulfill our Church callings. Day by day we quietly but surely become more like our Father in Heaven. With the help of the Spirit, we improve in one gospel area today and another gospel area tomorrow, until we find ourselves eventually striving to keep all of Heavenly Father's commandments. We slowly but surely turn our minds and hearts to God, and as we do our very nature is changed. We no longer desire to sin but desire instead "to do good continually." Each of us can receive hope from this statement by President Ezra Taft Benson: "The Lord is pleased with every effort, even the tiny, daily ones in which we strive to be more like Him. Though we may see that we have far to go on the road to perfection, we must not give up hope." (*Ensign,* October 1989, p. 5.)

A New Birth—Baptism

Baptism is the sign of the covenant that we make with Christ whereby we take upon us his name and become members of his church. It is the divinely appointed means of becoming clean and making us fit for the kingdom of heaven. Our souls must be cleansed of sin, for no unclean thing can enter the presence of God; baptism is a major part of the cleansing process. The water, of course, does not literally wash away our sins; however, obedience to the baptismal covenants keeps us clean before the Lord. Moroni stated: "And the first fruits of repentance is baptism; and baptism cometh by faith unto the fulfilling the commandments; and the fulfilling the commandments bringeth remission of sins" (Moroni 8:25).

Baptism is the entryway into the kingdom of God. Jesus taught that "except a man be born of water and of the Spirit, he cannot enter into the kingdom of God" (John 3:5). Repentance and baptism put us on the path to eternal life.

As we contemplate what baptism symbolizes, it is apparent why immersion is the only acceptable mode of baptism. The meaning of the word *baptism* during Jesus' time was "to bury or immerse." Baptism represents the burial and resurrection of Christ and also the death, resurrection, and eternal life of all those who sincerely participate in this ordinance. Referring to this symbolism, the Apostle Paul wrote: "We are buried with him by baptism into death: that like as Christ was raised up from the dead by the glory of the Father, even so we also should walk in newness of life. For if we have been planted together in the likeness of his death, we shall be also in the likeness of his resurrection." (Romans 6:4–5.)

Baptism also represents the death of an old way of life and a new birth into a more spiritual way of life. It is referred to as being born again, for through the ordinance of baptism we become sons and daughters of Christ.

As noted above, we need to be born of water and of the Spirit in order to enter the kingdom of God. Baptism is not complete without the reception of the Holy Ghost. The baptism of water begins the work of purification, and the baptism of the Spirit completes it. As Moroni explained:

> Baptism cometh by faith unto the fulfilling the commandments; and the fulfilling the commandments bringeth remission of sins;
>
> And the remission of sins bringeth meekness, and lowliness of heart; and because of meekness and lowliness of heart cometh the visitation of the Holy Ghost, which Comforter filleth with hope and perfect love, which love endureth by diligence unto prayer, until the end shall come, when all the saints shall dwell with God. (Moroni 8:25–26.)

The Baptism of the Savior

Nephi saw the baptism of Jesus in vision, and in 2 Nephi 31 shared some of the things we should understand about the Savior's baptism and about our own. Here are some of the important concepts he taught.

1. Though the Savior was unblemished and holy, he was baptized to fulfill all righteousness. Because we are unholy, we have a much greater need to be baptized. (Verse 5.)

2. Through his baptism, Jesus showed that he was willing to "[humble] himself before the Father, and [witness] unto the Father that he would be obedient unto him in keeping his commandments" (verse 7).

3. The Holy Ghost descended upon Jesus following his baptism. This should also take place sometime following our baptism. (Verse 8.)

4. The fact that the Savior was baptized shows the straitness of the path and the narrowness of the gate by which we all need to enter (verse 9).

5. Jesus has asked us to follow him. How indeed can we follow him unless we are willing to keep the commandments of the Father. (Verse 10.)

6. In order to receive the Holy Ghost and the baptism of fire, we need to follow the Son with "full purpose of heart, acting no hypocrisy and no deception before God, but with real intent, repenting of [our] sins, witnessing unto the Father that [we] are willing to take upon [us] the name of Christ, by baptism" (verse 13). This is much more than just being baptized when we turn eight years old because our parents want us to.

Baptism and Receiving the Holy Ghost Insufficient

Some have the mistaken understanding that baptism makes us automatic heirs of the celestial kingdom; rather, baptism simply puts us on the strait and narrow path that leads to eternal life. We still have to progress along the path until we reach the goal we are seeking. Nephi explained what we need to do to advance along the path: "Ye must press forward with a steadfastness in Christ, having a perfect brightness of hope, and a love of God and of all men. Wherefore, if ye shall press forward, feasting upon the word of Christ, and endure to the end, behold, thus saith the Father: Ye shall have eternal life." (2 Nephi 31:20.)

Notice the words Nephi uses to show that it takes real effort to move along the path: *press forward, steadfastness, hope, love, feasting,* and *endure.* There is no movement without action on our part. In fact, if we are not moving forward we are moving backward; lack of action causes us to backslide and eventually wander off the path. One person attempted to describe this truth by comparing the strait and narrow path to walking up a downward moving escalator. He said that we have to move our feet to get to the top; as soon as we stand still we begin to lose ground. Just to get through the gate, to start the game, to begin the trip, is not enough. Once we are on the path, we want to continue to learn and obey so we can enjoy everything God has prepared for us.

Chapter Seven

BECOMING
BORN AGAIN
Mosiah 1–5

Introduction

The focus of this chapter is spiritual conversion. Conversion is far more than just accepting the gospel or acquiring a testimony. Gospel conversion takes place when a person changes from a natural man to a spiritual person, from a fallen or carnal state to that of a Saint. This spiritual conversion is referred to as being born again because the old thoughts, desires, and beliefs are buried and replaced by a whole new way of thinking and of living. A person's very makeup and nature are quickened and changed through the workings of the Holy Ghost. This new birth takes place only as we receive and enjoy the companionship of the Holy Ghost and give ourselves completely to the Lord. The two conversion stories discussed in this chapter will help us better understand this conversion process and the marvelous blessings that accompany being born again.

King Benjamin's Address

When King Benjamin grew old, he wished to present his son Mosiah to his people as their new king and ruler. He also desired to help his people understand and appreciate the Savior better so they might be born again. An angel came to him and taught him about the Savior's future mortal life and atonement. The angel referred to his message of the Savior as the glad tidings of great joy. There is no doubt that Christ's atonement is the glad tidings of great joy—the good news that is the heart and core of the gospel. The angel came in answer to King Benjamin's prayers and righteousness; King Benjamin was then commanded to share the message with his people (see Mosiah 3:2–4). His message brought joy and rejoicing to the hearts of the Nephite people, and it will do the same for us as we accept and apply his teachings in our lives.

A proclamation was sent throughout all the land requesting the people to gather to the temple. So many people came that the record keepers could not number them. Therefore a tower was erected for Benjamin to stand on so he could be better seen and heard. His words were also written down and sent forth to those who could not hear him. (See Mosiah 2:1–8.)

The People Gather to the Temple

The scriptures indicate three different things the people desired to accomplish as they gathered at the temple: (1) they desired to hear the words that King Benjamin would speak to them; (2) they brought with them the firstlings of their flocks so they might offer sacrifice and burnt offerings according to the law of Moses; and (3) they desired to give thanks to the Lord for the many blessings he had bestowed upon them. (See Mosiah 2:1–4.) They probably had no idea of the great spiritual experience that awaited them.

These parallel three of the main reasons why we assemble each week in our places of worship. We desire to hear the word of God as it is taught from the scriptures and from the talks of latter-day prophets. Through partaking of the sacrament, we make covenants with God. And we thank God for his numerous blessings through testimony and prayer and song. When we worship the Lord with these three purposes in mind, our Sunday service becomes much more meaningful.

Attitude—an Important Part of Worship

All of us have probably had the experience of preparing a spiritual lesson or talk, only to find that those who were to be taught were not prepared to hear the sacred word of God. In such cases, we often have to water down the message that we prepared or not give it at all. The Savior taught that we should not cast our pearls before swine (see 3 Nephi 14:6) and warned that "that which cometh from above is sacred, and must be spoken with care, and by constraint of the Spirit" (D&C 63:64). When the people are not prepared for the word of God, the Spirit constrains the speaker to discuss things of lesser importance.

It is apparent by the way Benjamin started his discourse that he felt the sacred nature of his message and wanted to make sure that the people were prepared to listen: "I have not commanded you to come up hither to trifle with the words which I shall speak, but that you should hearken unto me, and open your ears that ye may hear, and your hearts that ye may understand, and your minds that the mysteries of God may be unfolded to your view" (Mosiah 2:9).

Service to Others Is Service to God

It seems as though King Benjamin desired to take the love and appreciation that the people felt for him and transfer it to the Savior. Therefore he began his talk with a discussion of service and how service to others is also service to God. After describing his own life of service, he declared: "I tell you these things that ye may learn wisdom; that ye may learn that when ye are in the service of your fellow beings ye are only in the service of your God" (Mosiah 2:17).

There is no better way to serve those around us than by serving their children and other family members. All parents are grateful to someone who has made a positive difference in the lives of their children. In this regard, God feels very much as we do. The best way to serve God is through service to his children.

Understanding our Indebtedness to God

Since humility precedes all spiritual growth, King Benjamin

desired that his people understand their deep indebtedness to God. He taught a series of ideas that can help each of us better understand just how much we owe our Father in Heaven and his Son Jesus Christ.

Idea one: Since he, as their king, had spent his life in their service, the people should be willing to serve one another (see Mosiah 2:18).

Idea two: His service to his people had really been service to God. If he as their earthly king deserved any thanks from them, then how much more ought they to thank their Heavenly King for the bounteous blessings he had given them (see Mosiah 2:19).

Idea three: Since God had created them, kept and preserved them, caused them to rejoice, granted them peace, and lent them breath from day to day so they could do according to their desires, if they served him with their whole souls they would still be unprofitable servants (see Mosiah 2:20–21).

Idea four: In return for his many blessings, all God required of the people was to keep his commandments; then, as soon as they kept his commandments, he blessed and prospered them. They were indebted to him for their lives, and as soon as they tried to pay him back by keeping his commandments, he immediately blessed them for their obedience. Therefore there was no way they could repay God for his goodness, and they would be indebted to him forever and ever. (See Mosiah 2:22–24.)

The Gift of the Atonement

Although Benjamin had given the people many reasons for feeling grateful to God, he had only been leading up to the main subject of his talk—the message that the angel had commanded him to give. It was now time to teach them about the Savior and his atonement—the gift that made it possible for them to return to God again (see Mosiah 3:5–17).

He told them that the Lord Omnipotent, who reigns from eternity to all eternity, would come down from heaven and dwell among men. He would work mighty miracles "such as healing the sick, raising the dead, causing the lame to walk, the blind to receive their sight, and the deaf to hear" (Mosiah 3:5).

Benjamin explained that this God among men would "suffer temptations, and pain of body, hunger, thirst, and fatigue, *even more than man can suffer, except it be unto death*" (Mosiah 3:7; emphasis added). He taught that his anguish for the sins of his people would be so great that he would bleed from every pore.

The Nephite people learned that this being would be called "Jesus Christ, the Son of God" and that his mother would be named Mary (Mosiah 3:8). They were taught concerning his death and resurrection, and they learned that because of his atonement they could repent and be saved in the kingdom of God. They learned that through the atonement of Christ, little children would be saved. They came to understand that "there shall be no other name given nor any other way nor means whereby salvation can come unto the children of men, only in and through the name of Christ, the Lord Omnipotent" (Mosiah 3:17).

Taking Advantage of the Atonement

King Benjamin then explained how all can take advantage of the Atonement. Partaking of the Atonement's blessings is the process of becoming a spiritual person—of putting off the natural man and becoming a Saint. It is the process of becoming spiritually born again.

> Men drink damnation to their own souls except they humble themselves and become as little children, and believe that salvation was, and is, and is to come, in and through the atoning blood of Christ, the Lord Omnipotent.
>
> For the natural man is an enemy to God, and has been from the fall of Adam, and will be, forever and ever, unless he yields to the enticings of the Holy Spirit, and putteth off the natural man and becometh a saint through the atonement of Christ the Lord, and becometh as a child, submissive, meek, humble, patient, full of love, willing to submit to all things which the Lord seeth fit to inflict upon him. (Mosiah 3:18–19.)

Becoming more like God is what rebirth is all about. This rebirth happens as we realize our great need for the Atonement and commit our lives to God. Through the help of Deity, our very nature can change: we can display such godly character traits as meekness, patience, and love. Those who heard Benjamin's talk responded to the Spirit and became impressive examples of what can happen in our own lives.

> When King Benjamin had made an end of speaking the words which had been delivered unto him by the angel of the Lord, . . . he cast his eyes round about on the multitude, and behold they had fallen to the earth, for the fear of the Lord had come upon them.
>
> And they had viewed themselves in their own carnal state, even less than the dust of the earth. And they all cried aloud with one voice, saying: O have mercy, and apply the atoning blood of Christ that we may receive forgiveness of our sins, and our hearts may be purified; for we believe in Jesus Christ, the Son of God, who created heaven and earth, and all things; who shall come down among the children of men.
>
> And it came to pass that after they had spoken these words the Spirit of the Lord came upon them, and they were filled with joy, having received a remission of their sins, and having peace of conscience, because of the exceeding faith which they had in Jesus Christ. . . .
>
> And they all cried with one voice, saying: Yea, we believe all the words which thou hast spoken unto us; and also, we know of their surety and truth, because of the Spirit of the Lord Omnipotent, which has wrought a mighty change in us, or in our hearts, that we have no more disposition to do evil, but to do good continually. (Mosiah 4:1–3; 5:2.)

The people had no more disposition to do evil for, through the workings of the Holy Ghost, the desires and intentions of their hearts had undergone a deep change. This mighty change of heart took place because they were completely sincere in their desire to be forgiven of their sins and to keep all of God's commandments.

Enos's Experience

Jacob, who was a younger brother of Nephi, was born in the wilderness. After Nephi died, Jacob became the leader of the Nephite people and became responsible for writing on the plates of Nephi. Just before his death, Jacob approached his son Enos and gave him the sacred charge of protecting and writing on these gold plates.

It looks as though Enos was a righteous man but had not as yet received the mighty change of heart that accompanies complete forgiveness of sin and spiritual rebirth. The extra responsibility of the plates seemed to weigh heavily upon Enos. One day while hunting in the forest, his focus shifted from hunting wild beasts to receiving a forgiveness for his sins. It is likely that what happened on this particular day was a culmination of many days of pondering and prayer.

Enos thanked God that his father was a just man and that he had taught him in the nurture and admonition of the Lord. For some reason, the words of his father sank deep into his heart. As you read the following verses, notice the action words that demonstrate the deep effort Enos made to be forgiven:

> And I will tell you of the wrestle which I had before God, before I received a remission of my sins.
>
> Behold, I went to hunt beasts in the forests; and the words which I had often heard my father speak concerning eternal life, and the joy of the saints, sunk deep into my heart.
>
> And my soul hungered; and I kneeled down before my Maker, and I cried unto him in mighty prayer and supplication for mine own soul; and all the day long did I cry unto him; yea, and when the night came I did still raise my voice high that it reached the heavens.
>
> And there came a voice unto me, saying: Enos, thy sins are forgiven thee, and thou shalt be blessed. (Enos 1:2–5.)

The voice he heard was the Lord speaking to his mind (see verse 10) and his "guilt was swept away" because of his "faith in Christ, whom [he had] never before heard nor seen" (Enos 1:6,8). As he received forgiveness of his sins, he found that his heart was filled with love for all people, and he immediately began to pray for the welfare of both the Nephites and the Lamanites.

Change of Heart Takes a Total Commitment to God

Forgiveness of sin and change of heart can only come when we are willing to give ourselves completely to the Savior and his teachings. Elder Robert L. Backman said that "we must voluntarily submit the process of molding and shaping of our characters to our Redeemer, who is, ultimately, the sculptor" (*BYU 1990–91 Devotional and Fireside Speeches* [Provo: BYU Press, 1991], p. 159). He then quoted the following paragraph from the writings of C. S. Lewis:

> Christ says "Give me All. I don't want so much of your time and so much of your money and so much of your work: I want You. I have not come to torment your natural self, but to kill it. No half-measures are any good. I don't want to cut off a branch here and a branch there, I want to have the whole tree down. . . . Hand over the whole natural self, all the desires which you think innocent as well as the ones you think wicked—the whole outfit. I will give you a new self instead. In fact, I will give you Myself: my own will shall become yours." (*Mere Christianity* [New York: Macmillan, 1960], p. 67.)

For most of us, spiritual rebirth is not an event but a process. We turn our hearts more and more toward God until eventually we are striving to keep all of God's commandments. We receive a greater and greater portion of the Holy Ghost in our lives until we are striving to do only what the Spirit asks us to do. Most people who have gone through the process of rebirth cannot identify any certain day that their heart was changed. They can only testify that they no longer desire to sin but desire to do good, serve others, and keep God's commandments. The time involved in the process of rebirth is very much determined by one's desire and commitment. The greater the commitment to be completely forgiven of our sins and have the constant companionship of the Holy Ghost, the faster our spiritual growth.

It is important to realize that spiritual growth (spiritual rebirth) does not call for fancy or unusual personal programs. We need only follow this simple formula described by numerous prophets:

1. Sincere, regular prayer.
2. Daily scripture study.
3. Striving to keep all of the commandments.
4. Service to others.

These four activities are the spiritual food that bring about spiritual growth. As we focus on serving others and God (instead of focusing on ourselves and our own spiritual growth), the growth we are seeking happens automatically. Although we may not notice it from day to day, as we look back we will see that significant change has taken place in our lives.

Chapter Eight

THE DOMINO
EFFECT
Mosiah 11–17

Introduction

In the Early 1900s a family joined the Church and prepared themselves to be sealed in the temple. One day at church they were seriously offended in front of the rest of the congregation. As the family walked home from the meetinghouse the children could see that their father was very upset and angry.

When they arrived home, the father asked the family to sit in a circle and remain silent until he was ready to speak. After twenty-five minutes of silence, the father's body relaxed and a quiet sob came from his lips. Tears started to trickle down his cheeks, and soon the whole family was crying. After telling each member of his family how much he loved him or her, the father said:

> I love all of you and I want us to be together, forever, as a family. And the only way that can be is for all of us to be good members of The Church of Jesus Christ of Latter-day Saints and be sealed by his holy priesthood in the temple. This is not the branch president's church. It is the Church of Jesus Christ. We will not let any man or any amount of hurt or embarrassment or pride keep us from being together forever. Next Sunday we will go back to church.

The family went back to church and was eventually sealed in the temple. The children grew up and were sealed to their own families. Today over one hundred members of this family are active in the Church because the father was willing to forgive and apply this great principle in his home. (See John H. Groberg, *Ensign,* May 1980, p. 49.)

Throughout this chapter we will refer to something called the domino effect—the effect that one person's actions have on others (such as the father's actions in this story). Nearly everyone knows what happens when a number of dominoes are lined up in a row and the first one is knocked over. Each succeeding domino falls until every domino has been affected, even though only the first domino was touched. Some people have set up tens of thousands of dominoes in intricate patterns and designs. The ripple effect from knocking over the first domino then travels in circles and up and down ramps, splits into several lines and comes together again, and finally, after fifteen or twenty minutes, the last domino finally falls. By touching just one domino, thousands of others are affected.

The domino effect is a common occurrence in the Church. Loving service can begin a chain of events that affects more and more lives until thousands of souls are changed for the better. Suppose that one young man decides to go on a mission. Let's say that ten people are converted and baptized through his efforts. These people become active and hold responsible Church positions, in which they affect the lives of many others. They teach their children the gospel, and their children serve missions and spread the gospel to still others. The children then marry, and the process continues. Meanwhile, those who have been taught teach their children and others until thousands enjoy the gospel in their lives. It is impossible to comprehend the number of people that might benefit from one simple act of kindness or one lesson or talk. Our service at church and at home has unlimited potential.

Abinadi and Alma

The domino effect has never been better illustrated than in the conversion of Alma the Elder. King Noah was the ruler over a group of Nephites in a land bordered by the Lamanites. He was a wicked man who not only committed grievous sins himself but also caused his people to rebel against God. Immorality and drunkenness became a way of life for Noah and his followers; furthermore, the people were forced to give a fifth part of all they owned to support Noah and his priests in their wickedness.

King Noah had replaced the original priests, who had been called of God, with men who were lifted up in the pride of their hearts and who loved to spend their time in riotous living. Most of the people followed their example and reveled in wickedness. When the prophet Abinadi warned the people that they needed to repent or they would be brought into bondage, they hardened their hearts against the word of God and sought to kill Abinadi.

Abinadi escaped on that occasion, but later he was again commanded by God to warn the people of their wickedness. This time he was imprisoned for prophesying of the destruction of the people and of the death of King Noah. When he was brought before Noah and his false priests, he courageously rebuked them for their corruption and wickedness and for teaching the people to sin. King Noah became angry and commanded the priests to have Abinadi killed, but as they attempted to lay their hands on him he withstood them and warned them that God would smite them if they tried to remove him before he had delivered the Lord's message. The Spirit of the Lord came upon Abinadi, and his face shone with "exceeding luster" (Mosiah 13:5). Abinadi then taught Noah and his priests of the atonement and the redemption of Jesus Christ.

When Abinadi had finished speaking, the king commanded his priests to take him and put him to death. One priest, however, a young man named Alma, believed Abinadi, and he began to plead with the king for Abinadi's life. The king became angry at Alma also—so much so that Alma had to flee for his life. Abinadi was then scourged and put to death by fire because "he would not deny the commandments of God" (Mosiah 17:20).

Abinadi may have gone to his death feeling that his obedience and service had had little impact on the people, but because of the domino effect his mission brought the gospel to thousands of souls. Although

Alma is the only person that the scriptures mention as being directly affected by Abinadi, think of the numerous people Alma helped in his lifetime. These people then taught the gospel to others, who taught it to others, and so on. There is no way to estimate how many thousands of people were blessed because of Abinadi's courage and his willingness to serve the Lord. And this number does not take into account the myriad people in this dispensation who have strengthened their own testimonies and spiritual resolve as they have read Abinadi's message as recorded in the Book of Mormon.

We Are All Connected

Sister Chieko N. Okazaki is the first counselor in the Relief Society general presidency. When Sister Okazaki was eleven years old, Sister Rosetta Colclough, a missionary in Hawaii, came to her junior high and invited all of the students to a special religion class taught at the LDS chapel near the school. Three other Japanese girls and Sister Okazaki, all Buddhists, accepted the invitation. This was her introduction to Christian instruction: four years later she joined the Church.

After she was called to the Relief Society general presidency, Sister Okazaki received a letter from Rosetta that contained an article Rosetta had written fifteen years earlier describing those religion classes:

> One day on the eleven o'clock period, only four [Japanese girls] came to class. I was very disappointed there were so few. . . . [But] near the close of the period, we stood in the little chapel with bowed heads and closed eyes, repeating in unison the Lord's Prayer. . . . As we prayed, I suddenly felt a bright light envelop us, coming from above like an inverted cone. A wonderful feeling of peace and joy filled my heart. I led the prayer very slowly as the bright light enfolded us. I was sure the girls felt it also, as their faces shone with an expression of deep reverence. We almost whispered "good-bye" so as not to break the spell, and they tiptoed out. I thought, "One or more of those girls will join the Church and become a great influence for good". . . .
>
> . . . [When] I heard your name announced by Sister Jack . . . I sat up straight and watched the TV screen eagerly and saw your name appear on the screen. Then you started to speak. The dark hair has turned to sil-

ver, but that sweet face was easily recognized. Yes, this is my little Chieko whom I taught at the Honomakau chapel in Kohala so many years ago. As I listened to your voice, tears of joy ran down my cheeks.

I thank my Heavenly Father that I had the privilege of teaching you about Jesus Christ our Savior in that little chapel . . . (Chieko N. Okazaki, *Ensign*, May 1993, pp. 84–85.)

Sister Colclough was disappointed at first when only four girls showed up for her religion class, but she did not realize at the time that one of them would be called by the Lord to preach the gospel throughout the world. Because of her deep love for others and her messages of kindness, service, and unity, Sister Okazaki has become one of the most beloved Church leaders of our time. Her impact on the lives of Church members is incalculable. Because of the domino effect, Rosetta's missionary class (where only four girls attended) has affected thousands of individuals.

Sister Okazaki described how we are all interconnected when she said:

Brothers and sisters, we never know how far the effects of our service will reach. We can never afford to be cruel or indifferent or ungenerous, because we are all connected, even if it is in a pattern that only God sees. I am part of the pattern. Rosetta is part of this pattern. You are part of this pattern. And the Savior is part of this pattern. In fact, I like to think that the Savior is the spaces in the pattern, for there would be no pattern at all without them. (*Ensign*, May 1993, p. 85.)

The Scope of Our Influence

The following comment was made by a convert to the Church in a ward sacrament meeting: "I am here because of a friend I had in junior high school. He was a good clean boy, and he believed in God. There was always something about him. It was as though he had something more to live for. I don't know where he is now, for we have lost touch, but I am here in this testimony meeting, a baptized member of the Church, because of him." (*Melchizedek Priesthood Personal Study Guide 2,* 1990, p. 123.)

This convert's story emphasizes the importance of striving to live the gospel and of applying the gospel principles in our association with others. It also demonstrated that we may never know of the influence for good we are having on those around us. Many seeds that are sown through righteousness and love take months and even years to come to fruition.

It is important to realize that the gospel of Jesus Christ works. Living the gospel and sharing it with others does change people's lives. Service in the kingdom does make a difference. God knows of the impact that our service and love has on the lives of others, and, as a loving father, he deeply appreciates our commitment and concern. Someday, if we remain righteous, we will know clearly of the impact for good that we have had on the lives of others.

Chapter Nine

MISSIONARY PRINCIPLES THAT WORK
Alma 17–26

Introduction

During their younger years, the sons of Mosiah, along with Alma the Younger, sought to destroy the Church. Following their conversion they traveled throughout the land of Zarahemla striving to repair the damage they had done to the Church. They then returned to King Mosiah and asked for permission to teach the gospel to the Lamanite people. After his sons had pleaded with him for many days, King Mosiah inquired of the Lord whether to allow his sons to go among the Lamanites. Mosiah's fears were calmed when the Lord said, "Let them go up, for many shall believe on their words, and they shall have eternal life; and I will deliver thy sons out of the hands of the Lamanites" (Mosiah 28:7).

Mosiah's reluctance is understandable, for the Lamanites were a "wild and a hardened and a ferocious people; a people who delighted in murdering the Nephites, and robbing and plundering them" (Alma 17:14). When the Nephites in Zarahemla heard that the sons of Mosiah were leaving to preach the gospel to the Lamanites, they laughed them to scorn and said, "Do ye suppose that ye can bring the Lamanites to the knowledge of the truth? Do ye suppose that ye can convince the Lamanites of the incorrectness of the traditions of their fathers, as stiffnecked a people as they are; whose hearts delight in the shedding of blood; whose days have been spent in the grossest iniquity; whose ways have been the ways of a transgressor from the beginning?" They suggested instead that the Nephites take up arms against the Lamanites and destroy them completely from the earth. (Alma 26:24; see also verses 23–25.)

In spite of the challenge they faced, the sons of Mosiah became the human instrument in converting thousands of Lamanites to Jesus Christ and his gospel. The principles that were effective for them will be just as effective for us as we apply them in our missionary and activation efforts.

Personal Preparation

A careful reading of Doctrine and Covenants section 11 suggests that effective missionary work takes personal preparation. One mission president indicated that in his mission eighty percent of the work and success came from twenty percent of the missionaries. He attributed this to the preparation and worthiness of these missionaries. Some missionaries are ready to teach from the moment they enter the mission field, while others, because of their lack of preparation, take months and even a year or more to become effective. As we read the following three case studies, note the different levels of preparation and therefore the different levels of effectiveness each missionary brought with him as he entered the mission field.

1. Mark had lied to everyone who interviewed him for his mission. He did not want anyone to know about the serious sins he had been involved in and felt that the Lord would forgive him if he stopped doing them before he left for the mission field.

2. Allan had planned on a mission all his life but had done little to actually prepare for it. He seldom read the scriptures, and, although he prayed regularly, his prayers were mainly vain repetitions that he had heard others use. He attended church but seldom participated or became involved in the lessons.

3. Rick felt worthy to go on a mission. He had studied the stan-

dard works regularly and had received a personal testimony through meaningful prayer. He had come to understand and appreciate the loving atonement of the Savior and could hardly wait to be able to share the good news with others.

It is apparent that of these three young men only Rick is in a position to receive the guidance of the Holy Ghost and make an immediate impact in the mission field. Allan will first have to convert himself and learn the gospel, and Mark should not even be going. As a matter of fact, if Mark's dishonesty and past sins become known, he will be sent home. Serious transgression might even prevent someone from serving a mission, and certainly potential missionaries must demonstrate an ability to live the commandments—and therefore be eligible to receive the Spirit—before serving a mission.

The same principles of preparation and righteousness are just as necessary in our member missionary efforts. God wants every young man to serve a formal full-time mission, but he also expects all members to be actively involved in missionary work. Our effectiveness greatly increases as we prepare ourselves and receive the promptings of the Holy Spirit. As we read about the sons of Mosiah, we see that there were three main things that they did to better prepare themselves for missionary work. The first two are identified in the following scripture: "For they were men of a sound understanding and they had searched the scriptures diligently, that they might know the word of God. But this is not all; they had given themselves to much prayer, and fasting; therefore they had the spirit of prophecy, and the spirit of revelation, and when they taught, they taught with power and authority of God." (Alma 17:2–3.)

This matches what the Lord told his latter-day people: "Seek not to declare my word, but first seek to obtain my word, and then shall your tongue be loosed; then, if you desire, you shall have my Spirit and my word, yea, the power of God unto the convincing of men" (D&C 11:21).

Through consistent scripture study and sincere personal prayer, we can come to understand the gospel and prepare ourselves spiritually to receive the Holy Ghost. Once we have the Holy Ghost with us we are in a position to share the gospel with others, for it is by the power of the Holy Ghost that men and women come to know the gospel is true. In fact, in Doctrine and Covenants 50, the Lord indicates that we should not teach his gospel unless we do have his Spirit. In this section he declares that we have been called to "preach [his] gospel by the Spirit" and that if we teach his gospel without the Spirit, it is not of him (see D&C 50:13–20). Regular scripture study and prayer make us receptive to the promptings of the Spirit.

The third thing that made the sons of Mosiah such tremendous missionaries was their realization of the worth of a soul. Through their conversion and obedience, they came to realize the value of every human being. They had felt the joy that comes from forgiveness of sin, and they desired that every person should feel this great joy. The great love that they had for all of the children of God is described well in the following two verses of scripture:

> Now they were desirous that salvation should be declared to every creature, for they could not bear that any human soul should perish; yea, even the very thoughts that any soul should endure endless torment did cause them to quake and tremble.
>
> And thus did the Spirit of the Lord work upon them, for they were the very vilest of sinners. And the Lord saw fit in his infinite mercy to spare them; nevertheless they suffered much anguish of soul because of their iniquities, suffering much and fearing that they should be cast off forever. (Mosiah 28:3–4.)

Elder H. Burke Peterson told of a young man who demonstrated this great desire to share the gospel with others. As Elder Peterson was concluding a meeting with a stake presidency in another country, a knock came on the door and someone handed an envelope with Elder Peterson's name on it to the stake president. The letter inside introduced Elder Peterson to a young man who needed an interview in order to be accepted as a missionary.

As soon as the meeting was over, Elder Peterson invited the young man to join him. Elder Peterson's first impression was one of shock. The young man was unshaven, his clothes were wrinkled, he smelled of cigarette smoke, and he had a rolled-up paperback book in his hand. He certainly did not look like someone who was preparing to serve the Lord on a mission.

However, as Elder Peterson shook the young man's hand and looked into his eyes, he could tell that here was a young man of exceptional quality. The young man excused his appearance and said that he had spent the last thirteen hours on the bus. This accounted for his rumpled appearance and the smell of cigarette smoke, and Elder Peterson noticed that the paperback book was a well-read copy of the Book of Mormon. Elder Peterson explained what happened next:

> He went on to say that three years ago he had joined the Church because of his association with our young people. He said they were different. His parents had given him permission if he wanted to, but warned that if he did, he would no longer have a bed in their home. He could no longer live with them as their son.
>
> When he was baptized, his father kept his word and opened the back door, telling him never to return. The young man didn't. He moved in with friends. He told me that for the past three years he had been working and going to school. He said he had saved over $2,000 to keep himself on a mission. Please, could he go, he said; he wanted to more than anything in the world. The impression of the Spirit said yes, and he's now part of the army of . . . stalwarts who are out covering the earth as servants of the Master. (H. Burke Peterson, *Ensign*, November 1974, p. 68.)

Like the sons of Mosiah and this young man, as we strive to put God first in our lives the Spirit of the Lord will fill our hearts with love and we will begin to appreciate the value of each individual. We too will then desire to share the gospel with those around us so they can partake of the blessings that we enjoy. Once we have the guidance of the Holy Ghost, we are ready to use the principles of missionary work that worked so well for the sons of Mosiah. As we study these principles, however, it is essential to remember that only the Spirit can carry the gospel message to the hearts of those we are striving to help. There is little effective missionary work without the Spirit.

Patience and Example in Afflictions

The Lord knew that as the sons of Mosiah attempted to teach the gospel to the Lamanites they would suffer much affliction. He also knew that how they handled this affliction would be a key to converting many people; therefore, he gave them the following counsel: "Go forth among the Lamanites, thy brethren, and establish my word; yet ye shall be patient in long-suffering and afflictions, that ye may show forth good examples unto them in me, and I will make an instrument of thee in my hands unto the salvation of many souls" (Alma 17:11).

While serving a full-time mission as a young man, Elder Hugh B. Brown illustrated the importance of patience and persistence. He had gone to a certain house several times and had been rejected and warned not to come back again, but he kept returning because he was prompted to do so by the Spirit. One day, as he was attempting to walk by the house, the Spirit again prompted him to knock on the door. He could see a woman in the front room knitting; when she refused to answer the door, he went around to the back door. Since there was no knocker on the back door, he proceeded to knock with his walking stick and did so with considerable vigor.

This brought the woman to the door in a hurry, and she didn't arrive with a smile on her face. Elder Brown quickly apologized for interrupting her and told her that he had come over six thousand miles to bring her a message that the Lord wanted her to have. She was amazed that the Lord had a message for her and consented to listen to what Elder Brown had to say. He told her of the restoration of the gospel and Jesus' Church. She was impressed with the message. He did not have an opportunity to teach her further, for a few days later he returned to Canada.

Ten years later he returned to England as a soldier. This same woman and her daughters were at a church meeting he attended. She thanked him for his patience and persistence, saying: "I do thank God and thank you that you came to my door with that message many years ago. I and my daughters joined the Church . . . , and we thank God that you had the courage, the fortitude, and the faith to come to me with that divine message and to leave it with me in the name of the Lord." (*Ensign,* July 1972, p. 86.)

Because Elder Brown did not allow threats and rejection to drive the Spirit out of his heart, he was able to respond to the Spirit and say the things that this sister needed to hear. All of us will suffer some rejection and embarrassment, if not outright ridicule, as we strive to share the gospel with others. How we handle this rejection is an important part of our missionary effort. As we exemplify Christ even in negative situations, hearts will be touched and doors will be opened.

A Lifetime of Service

After the sons of Mosiah and some of their friends reached the land of Nephi (where the Lamanites lived), Ammon blessed them. They then divided and went their separate ways. Ammon was led by the Lord to the land of Ishmael, where he was bound and taken before King Lamoni. When King Lamoni asked Ammon what his desires were, he answered: "I desire to dwell among this people for a time; yea, and perhaps until the day I die" (Alma 17:23). This pleased Lamoni, who not only had Ammon's bands loosed but invited him to marry one of his daughters. Ammon politely refused the offer, then asked if he could instead become one of King Lamoni's servants. He was assigned to join some other servants in watching the king's flocks.

He had served the king only three days when another group of Lamanites attacked and scattered the king's flocks. The king's servants began to fear for their lives, for he had slain previous servants who had been tending the flocks when they were scattered.

Ammon's love for all people is clearly manifested in this story as his heart went out to these servants whom he considered "to be his brethren" (Alma 17:30). Although he was the son of a king, he felt himself no better than these Lamanite servants. With the Spirit of the Lord he stepped forward and defended the king's flocks, during the course of the battle slaying six Lamanites with his sling, killing the Lamanite leader, and cutting off the arm of every Lamanite who raised his sword against him. Feeling that the king would not believe what had taken place, Ammon's fellowservants gathered up the arms of the Lamanites and carried them into the king as a testimony of what Ammon had done. Ammon showed such power and courage that the servants felt he might even be the Great Spirit.

However, it was not Ammon's great power or courage that impressed the king the most—it was his faithful and loyal service. When Lamoni asked where Ammon was, he was told that he was preparing the king's horses and chariots for his upcoming trip to visit his father. When King Lamoni heard this he was astonished and said: "Surely there has not been any servant among all my servants that has been so faithful as this man; for even he doth remember all my commandments to execute them" (Alma 18:10). He then sent for Ammon and listened to the gospel message that Ammon had been waiting to share with him.

This same commitment to service was demonstrated in our day by a young missionary named Nolan Bergeson. He came in contact with a nonmember woman who was deaf but often attended church. For years she had expressed a desire to be baptized, but the mission rule was that all converts had to be taught the six missionary lessons before baptism. She could only communicate by sign language, and since none of the missionaries knew the sign language of the deaf, she had never been taught.

Elder Bergeson was not an academic giant, but he was committed to serving the Lord and to serving others. He met with this good woman and received from her a copy of the signs of the alphabet. That night he memorized the sign for each letter of the alphabet. The next day, during the course of six hours, he taught her the entire first missionary lesson, spelling each word to her and watching patiently as she spelled back the answer to each question.

Elder Bergeson was not satisfied with the way the first discussion had gone, so he went to the library and borrowed some books on sign language. He practiced continually and each discussion became easier and more meaningful. The last discussion took only a little more time than it would have if both participants had been speaking audibly. The sister was baptized; thereafter, in nonverbal communication, she has blessed Elder Bergeson's name for his great willingness to serve. Numerous elders had an opportunity to serve this wonderful lady, but none of them were willing to pay the extra price of time and effort until Elder Bergeson came along. (See Steven A. Wolfe, *Ensign,* August 1978, p. 66.)

Another important concept that Ammon taught concerning service is that it is a lifetime commitment. He was committed to spending the rest of his life with the Lamanites. He and his brothers served a fourteen-year mission and only left when, along with their converts, they had to flee for their lives.

When we were baptized, each of us made the promise that we would "stand as witnesses of God at all times and in all things, and in all places that [we] may be in, even until death" (Mosiah 18:9). This is our commitment to full-time service. Sometimes we work with someone for a few days, weeks, or months, and then become discouraged and look for someone else to help. Like Ammon, we need to be willing to serve someone perhaps even "until the day [we] die" (Alma 17:23–24). When people have initially rejected our gospel message and we continue to serve and befriend them, they come to realize that our desire to serve and help them is sincere.

Foundation of Missionary Work

When King Lamoni heard that Ammon's brothers were in prison in the land of Middoni, he volunteered to go with Ammon for the purpose of seeking their release. As they were traveling to Middoni, they met Lamoni's father, who was the king over all of the Lamanites. He demanded to know why Lamoni was traveling with a Nephite—"one of the children of a liar." After listening to Lamoni's conversion story, the father became very angry and demanded that Lamoni kill Ammon with his sword. When Lamoni refused to slay Ammon, his father drew his sword that he might smite Lamoni to the earth.

Ammon interceded and told the king that he should not slay his son: Lamoni was an innocent man and murdering him could lead to the king losing his soul. This so enraged the king that he attempted to kill Ammon instead, but Ammon withstood and defeated him. Once the king realized Ammon could kill him, he pleaded with Ammon: he would give Ammon anything he desired up to half of his kingdom if he would spare his life. But Ammon only asked for two things: that his brothers be released from prison and that Lamoni retain his kingdom. The marvelous effect that sincere love can have on missionary work is easily recognized in what happened next:

> And when he saw that Ammon had no desire to destroy him, and when he also saw the *great love* he had for his son Lamoni, he was astonished exceedingly, and said: Because this is all that thou hast desired, . . . I will grant unto you that my son may retain his kingdom from this time and forever; and I will govern him no more—
>
> And I will also grant unto thee that thy brethren may be cast out of prison, and thou and thy brethren may come unto me, in my kingdom; for I shall greatly desire to see thee. For the king was greatly astonished at the words which he had spoken, and also at the words which had been spoken by his son Lamoni, *therefore he was desirous to learn them.* (Alma 20:26–27; emphasis added.)

The pure love that comes through the Spirit is just as powerful today as it was at the time of Ammon. Two missionaries received a letter from a man and his family requesting that they come by and pick up the Book of Mormon they had given the family. Although they had been taught several discussions, the family had decided that they were no longer interested in learning more about the Church.

One of the elders was shy and possessed few discussion skills, but the other elder was outgoing and persuasive and felt that, through the use of these talents, he would be able to change the father's mind. While the outgoing elder used every persuasive skill he could think of, the other elder just listened. Finally the father agreed to continue the missionary discussions. It wasn't until later that the elders found out what changed the man's mind.

> At the family's baptism, the talented elder remembered the night with some degree of pride. After the baptism the man told him, "The night I changed my mind and continued to have you teach me was the most important night of my life. As you talked to me, my mind was so

determined to not listen that there was nothing you could have said that would have caused me to continue. But then I looked at your companion. His eyes were focused on me. I saw in his face more love than I'd ever known before. My heart felt a spirit that made it so I could not resist his silent message. I decided then that if this church could cause someone to love like that, then I wanted to be part of it." (Devin G. Durrant, *Ensign*, May 1984, p. 37.)

Friendship

One of the things that caused Lamoni to listen to Ammon was the testimonies born by his servants of Ammon's loyalty and dedication to the king. Based on the things they had seen Ammon say and do, they said to the king: "Therefore, we know that he is a friend to the king" (Alma 18:3). Friendship cultivates confidence and trust, which allows the gospel to be presented in a climate of fellowship and warmth. Lamoni was willing to listen to Ammon because he trusted him. Sometimes we become too eager to teach the gospel and don't spend the time it takes to develop sincere friendship. One of the main missionary responsibilities of Church members is to become friends with those they work with, live with, or play with. An example of the force for good that just being friendly can produce was shared in a letter to the editor written by Danny Reynolds, the University of Miami varsity cheerleading coach.

A few years ago Brigham Young University won the national football championship. One of the major reasons for this was their win over the then top-rated University of Miami. However, more important than the win or the championship was the friendship the BYU cheerleaders offered to the cheerleaders from Miami.

In his letter to the BYU student newspaper, the Miami cheerleading coach indicated that in spite of the loss it was one of the best weekends his squad had experienced. He talked about all the wonderful things the BYU cheerleaders did to make their stay in Provo enjoyable, including transportation and a driver, a special dinner, accompanying them to a dance, a night tour of Provo, and caring assistance when one of their cheerleaders suffered a minor head injury. Talking about the head injury, the coach said that he had never seen so many people so genuinely concerned.

He closed his letter with the following comments:

> I appreciated the trip so much, primarily because your cheerleaders shared their faith with my kids.
>
> . . . Sharing your faith with us made us all look a little closer at our personal relationship with Christ.
>
> We all felt like we made great friends on the trip. . . .
>
> I've started reading the Book of Mormon, Another Testament of Jesus Christ. (Danny Reynolds, Miami varsity cheerleading coach, *Daily Universe* Letters to the Editor, September 19, 1990.)

The BYU cheerleaders may never know how many of their friends from Miami will respond to the gospel and join the Church, but they did their part by becoming friends and sharing their testimonies with them. Because of their mutual friendship, the Miami cheerleaders will probably be more receptive to missionaries and other Church members. Seeds have been planted that others can help nourish and grow.

A Non-threatening Approach

A man named Sharman Hummell, who lived in the eastern United States, was traveling by bus to San Francisco. When the bus stopped in Salt Lake City, a Primary girl boarded the bus and sat next to him. She was going to Reno, Nevada, to visit her aunt. As they traveled through Utah, Sharman noticed a sign inviting people to visit the Mormon Sunday School and he asked the girl if she was a Mormon.

When she said that she was, he asked her what Mormons believed. He was totally unprepared for the answer he received. The little girl recited the first article of faith and talked about it. She continued with the second article of faith and the third until she had recited and explained all thirteen articles of faith. By the time she got off the bus in Reno, Sharman was profoundly impressed.

The rest of the way to San Francisco he pondered about this little girl and what could possibly prompt her to know her doctrine so well. The first thing he did after arriving in San Francisco was look up the Church in the yellow pages. Two missionaries were sent to where he was staying, and he and his family became members of the Church. His only regret is that he never asked her name so he has not been able to thank her for what she did for him and his family. (Thomas S. Monson, *Ensign,* April 1994, pp. 67–68.)

One of the reasons why Sharman responded so willingly was that the little girl presented the gospel in a totally nonthreatening manner. Sometimes we make the mistake of arguing the gospel with our husband, wife, friend, or co-worker. This creates a threatening relationship in which accepting the gospel means the person has to lose face or admit that he was wrong. It is often better to live the gospel and allow those with whom we associate to initiate discussions about the Church. If we answer their questions by discussing the truths of the gospel in a clear and simple way and avoid challenging their beliefs, they will feel comfortable in initiating future gospel discussions. Ammon seemed to understand this principle well, for he waited until the king almost begged to be taught before he formally taught him the gospel. As a matter of fact, the king said, "If thou wilt tell me concerning these things, whatsoever thou desirest I will give unto thee" (Alma 18:21). The scripture then indicates that Ammon, "being wise, yet harmless," began to teach Lamoni the gospel (Alma 18:22).

Ammon did not challenge Lamoni's beliefs but instead added to the truths he already understood. The following dialogue is a good example of the nonthreatening approach Ammon used with Lamoni.

And Ammon began to speak unto him with boldness, and said unto him: Believest thou that there is a God?

And he answered, and said unto him: I do not know what that meaneth.

And then Ammon said: Believest thou that there is a Great Spirit?

And he said, Yea.

And Ammon said: This is God. And Ammon said unto him again: Believest thou that this Great Spirit, who is God, created all things which are in heaven and in the earth?

> And he said: Yea, I believe that he created all things which are in the earth; but I do not know the heavens. (Alma 18:24–29.)

By starting with something both agreed on, Ammon was able to lead Lamoni into new gospel truths. Many "wise, yet harmless" missionaries in South America use this same approach when questions concerning the worship of Saints are asked. Many South Americans have been raised in a religion in which Saints play a major role. Instead of speaking negatively of this belief in saints, these missionaries talk about our own belief in Saints and point out that the official name of the Church is The Church of Jesus Christ of Latter-day Saints. They talk about how Heavenly Father wants all of us to become Saints.

Instead of challenging the custom of praying to or through Saints, the missionaries talk about this idea of praying through someone or in the name of someone and help these people come to understand that they should pray to Heavenly Father through Jesus Christ. They make adjustments to the people's understanding rather than destroying what they believe in and trying to teach them from scratch. With the Lord's help, we can always locate some common ground from which to begin teaching.

Never Give Up

Working with nonmembers and members who are less-active can sometimes become discouraging. When we don't experience any success for a while, we can become disheartened and give up on those with whom we are working. When we are experiencing these feelings, a good place to turn for comfort and inspiration is Alma 26:27–33. In these verses, Ammon explains the discouragement and the eventual blessings that came because he and his brethren never gave up. Here are just a few lines from these verses:

> Now when our hearts were depressed, and we were about to turn back, behold, the Lord comforted us, and said: Go amongst thy brethren, the Lamanites, and bear with patience thine afflictions, and I will give unto you success. . . .

And we have suffered all manner of afflictions, and all this, that perhaps we might be the means of saving some soul; and we supposed that our joy would be full if perhaps we could be the means of saving some.

Now behold, we can look forth and see the fruits of our labors; and are they few? I say unto you, Nay, they are many; yea, and we can witness of their sincerity, because of their love towards their brethren and also towards us. (Alma 26:27, 30–31.)

It is easier to be patient in our missionary labors when we remember that we are serving a life-long mission. This important truth was explained well by Elder John H. Groberg: "We must stop trying to separate missionary work from life. Missionary work is life—living is a mission; life is a mission; we are all on a lifelong mission." (*Ensign*, July 1980, p. 9.)

Elder Groberg went on to explain that the things we do each day of our lives influence people to draw closer to God or to move further away from him. He told of a man whom he sat next to on an airplane and who asked him what he did for a living. When he told him that he was a Mormon missionary, the man answered that he didn't have much use for missionaries or others who went around "trying to get people to change their minds." Elder Groberg describes the discussion that then took place.

I said, "Well, you're a missionary!" He emphatically denied this and asked why I said he was. I told him that everything he did and said influenced others one way or the other, so he was a missionary for his way of life.

"For example?" he queried.

"Well," I replied, "I see by the packet of cigarettes in your pocket that you believe in smoking. Your children see you smoking and are influenced to smoke also when they are able. You are thus doing missionary work for the tobacco people". . . .

Needless to say, we had a very interesting discussion the rest of the trip. But the point here is: We are all missionaries. All of our words and actions have eternal consequences—for they influence not only ourselves, but others as well. (*Ensign*, July 1980, p. 9.)

It is sobering to ponder the influence we have had and will have on those we come in contact with. Since we cannot avoid influencing the lives of others in some way, we might as well make the decision to influence them for the good. As we set good examples and look for opportunities to share the gospel with others, the methods used by the sons of Mosiah will be of great help to us. The key will be to live in such a way that we can receive direction and guidance from the Holy Ghost. With the Lord's help, we can be successful in sharing the gospel with others.

Chapter Ten

PRINCIPLES OF
PROPER WORSHIP
Alma 31

Introduction

The Zoramites were a group of Nephites who had separated themselves from the rest of the Nephite people. When Alma heard that the
Zoramites were perverting the teachings of God, his "heart was
exceedingly sorrowful" (Alma 31:2). He gathered together several
other missionaries, including two of his sons, and departed for the
land where the Zoramites lived. When they arrived, Alma and his
companions were astonished at how far the Zoramites had strayed
from the truths that they once had understood. Some of these perver-
sions follow:

1. The synagogues the Zoramites had built contained a stand in
the center that would admit only one person at a time. Whosoever
desired to worship had to climb to the top of the stand, stretch forth his
hands towards heaven, and with a loud voice pray the same identical
prayer as everyone else did.

2. The prayer said that God was a spirit, that the Zoramites had
been separated from their brethren because they were elected and chosen, and that there would be no Christ. It stated that the Zoramites had
been elected to be saved because they were a chosen and a holy

people, while everyone else would be cast down to hell. It offered appreciation that they were not led away after the "foolish traditions" that bound others to a belief in Christ.

4. After each person had offered this prayer, he returned to his home and never spoke of God again until a week later when he next came to the synagogue.

5. The Zoramites' hearts were set on gold, silver, and all manner of fine clothing and goods. They were proud and boastful and would not allow the poor to enter their synagogues. The poor felt that the only place a person could worship was in a synagogue; therefore, they believed they could not worship God.

Humility and Prayer

Two of the most serious flaws in Zoramite worship were their lack of humility and their inappropriate prayer. Pride had replaced humility in many hearts, and it is apparent from their established prayer that they had drifted far from the sincere prayer taught by God and his prophets. Without humility and heartfelt prayer, which are the very center of effective worship, their worship was ineffective, for it lacked both spirit and substance.

The Zoramites who were filled with pride refused to listen to Alma, but those who had been humbled by their afflictions were prepared to hear the word of God. Alma told them that it was a blessing to them that they had been cast out and rejected, for it had brought them to a lowliness of heart (see Alma 32:12–13).

Alma emphasized the importance of humility when he said: "And now, . . . because ye were compelled to be humble ye were blessed, do ye not suppose that they are more blessed who truly humble themselves because of the word? Yea, he that truly humbleth himself, and repenteth of his sins, and endureth to the end, the same shall be blessed—yea, much more blessed than they who are compelled to be humble because of their exceeding poverty." (Alma 32:14–15.)

Humility's crucial nature was explained by Mormon when he taught that meekness and lowliness of heart bring the Holy Ghost, "which Comforter filleth with hope and perfect love" (see Moroni

8:26). When we are humble and teachable, we hearken to the counsel of our leaders and to the promptings of the Spirit. Our hearts are submissive and obedient to the Savior and his teachings. The effect that widespread humility would have on the world is alluded to in the following words of President Howard W. Hunter:

> And what of the meek? In a world too preoccupied with winning through intimidation and seeking to be number one, no large crowd of folk is standing in line to buy books that call for mere meekness. But the meek shall inherit the earth, a pretty impressive corporate takeover—and done *without* intimidation! Sooner or later, and we pray sooner *than* later, everyone will acknowledge that Christ's way is not only the *right* way, but ultimately the *only* way to hope and joy. Every knee shall bow and every tongue will confess that gentleness is better than brutality, that kindness is greater than coercion, that the soft voice turneth away wrath. (*Ensign*, May 1993, pp. 64–65.)

Humility puts us in a position to receive answers to our prayers; humility increases receptiveness to what God wants us to do. Unlike the Zoramite prayers, our prayers should change as our circumstances change. Prayer is an opportunity to personally communicate with our Father in Heaven. It is a time that we can really talk out our problems and concerns with him and share with him our insecurities and joys, our doubts and desires. This type of personal prayer—one-on-one if you will—takes pondering and preparation. It requires that we think about the feelings we want to share with God and carefully consider the areas in which we need his help. During these pre-prayer moments, we silently ask that the Spirit might be with us as we pray so that our desires may be in tune with the desires of the Lord. This type of prayer becomes a consistent pattern of meaningful worship, for it helps us to love him, to appreciate him, and to seek to be like him.

Sabbath Services

A Primary presidency, recognizing a need for increased reverence, taught the children a song containing the following words:

> This is God's house
> And he is here today
> He hears each song of praise,
> And listens when we pray.
>   (*Sing with Me,* A–6.)

A little boy named Jody was impressed with this song and asked several questions about it. He arrived at the conclusion that, since God was in the building, all he had to do to find him was to search every room in the building. When Sister Mary Dyer heard this story, it made her search her own heart concerning her faith. She asked herself, "Have I ever gone into the meetinghouse with the purpose of searching for God?" After she had pondered this question, another question came to her mind: "Have I ever gone with an abiding and unwavering faith that I would indeed find him there?" She realized that she had to answer no to both questions. Her church attendance had become mechanical.

As she began to prepare herself to search for God in her meetings, she began to consistently feel the Spirit of God in his house. She later explained what happened as she listened to those who spoke, participated in classroom discussions, and sang hymns of praise and devotion: "I saw the Spirit working everywhere: in the sacrament prayer, in the smallest deacon passing the sacrament, in the young sister who left a small cluster of close friends to sit beside a lonely stranger, in the young brother who, after the meeting, guided his lovely girl friend to a corner to keep an elderly woman company while she waited for her ride home."

She came to realize that love, reverence, and devotion brought the Spirit and that she had a responsibility to others—and to herself—to emulate these virtues. Unlike the Zoramites, who never thought of God during the week, Mary found that her weekday activities had a direct effect on her Sunday worship, for how could she "be harsh in judgment or unkind in thought or deed throughout the week if [she expected] to return to His house on Sunday, look for Him there, and find Him?" (See Mary E. Dyer, *Ensign,* October 1981, p. 45.)

We can each find God in our services if we come in an attitude of worship and if we participate in the songs, prayers, and lessons. Worshiping is more than just listening. It includes desiring to draw closer to God and to share our love for him. It includes enthusiastically singing praises to his name and remembering and appreciating the Savior as we reverently partake of the sacrament. It includes centering our talks and lessons around the Savior and his teachings. President Spencer W. Kimball said that worship "is an individual responsibility, and regardless of what is said from the pulpit, if one wishes to worship the Lord in spirit and in truth, he may do so" (*Ensign,* January 1978, p. 5).

Worship the True and Living God

Elder Bruce R. McConkie stated that "there is probably more misinformation and error [concerning how to worship the Lord] than in any other area in the entire world, and yet there is no other thing as important as knowing who and how we should worship" (*Ensign,* December 1971, p. 129).

The Lord has told us that we should love and serve him, "the only living and true God, and that he should be the only being whom [we] should worship" (D&C 20:19). He has said that we must worship him with all of our might, mind, and strength—with our whole soul (see 2 Nephi 25:29). God revealed that we need to know how to worship and know what to worship in order to come to the Father and in due time receive of his fulness (see D&C 93:19). He has indicated that "they who worship him, must worship in spirit and in truth" (JST, John 4:26; see also verses 22–26).

These scriptures teach us three important principles concerning worship: (1) we need to worship the true and living God; (2) we need to worship the Lord with the power of the Spirit; (3) we need to worship God in the correct manner with our whole heart and soul.

The following statement by Elder McConkie emphasizes the importance of worshiping the true and living God: "There is no salvation in worshiping a false god. It does not matter one particle how sincerely someone may believe that God is a golden calf, or that he is an immaterial, uncreated power that is in all things; the worship of such a being or concept has no saving power." (*Ensign*, December 1971, p. 129.)

The Zoramite worship was doomed from its beginning because they worshiped a God of their own making and they did so without the Spirit of God. A God does not have to be fashioned from wood or stone in order to be false. When we consider the popular Christian idea of a God without "body, parts, or passions," it is easy to see why Jesus told Joseph Smith that all of the Christian creeds were wrong. (JS—H 1:19.)

Worshiping God in spirit and truth go hand in hand, for only through the Spirit can we come to know and worship the true God. The more we learn about God and his gospel, the better we can worship him. Those who truly seek to worship God will be directed by the Spirit to the true and living God—unlike the dead gods, who have no power to bless or save. Because of his compassion, kindness, and love, to know God is to love him and to want to be like him.

Service

Quiet acts of service are an important way of worshiping God. Steven learned this important truth from a sister in his ward whom he refers to as the Flower Sister. He entered the chapel early one Sabbath morning and saw her slipping out the other door of the chapel. He knew it was the Flower Sister because a beautiful floral arrangement had been placed near the podium. He felt almost as if he had intruded upon a sacred act, for every week the Flower Sister arranges her flowers "beautifully and imaginatively—and anonymously."

This sister rarely uses expensive greenhouse blooms. Some weeks she gathers goldenrod, wild daisies, tall grasses, and cattails and arranges them in beautiful ways. Steven sometimes wonders if the Flower Sister knows how much her weekly offering means to him—how much her silent, delicate contribution adds to his day's worship. He sometimes wishes to thank her for what she does, but he knows that compliments are not the reason she brings the flowers each week. He's sure she would keep bringing them even if no one noticed. Says Steven: "She has taught me that a kindness done with no thought of public recognition is a form of silent worship. . . . I continue to look forward every Sunday to her prayer of flowers." (Steven L. Orton, *Ensign,* April 1994, p. 17.)

True Worship—Seven Days a Week

Genuine worship is closely tied to obedience. It begins with faith in God and Jesus Christ and an acceptance and acknowledgment of the fact that they live. We worship God when we repent of our sins and strive to keep his commandments. We demonstrate worship as we help the poor, visit the sick, and embrace such qualities as mercy, brotherly kindness, humility, patience, and charity. We worship the Lord when we marry in the temple, teach our children the gospel, and honor our own father and mother. To worship the Lord is much more than prayer and song and church attendance. It is to do everything we can do to keep his commandments and to build up his kingdom here on the earth. It is to show our love for him by striving to become like him. It is to place him first in our lives.

Chapter Eleven

PRINCIPLES OF PRAYER
Alma 34

Why Pray?

As Amulek teaches, prayer can give us the power to resist the temptations of the devil: "Yea, and I also exhort you, my brethren, that ye be watchful unto prayer continually, that ye may not be led away by the temptations of the devil, that he may not overpower you, that ye may not become his subjects at the last day; for behold, he rewardeth you no good thing" (Alma 34:39).

Talking about his home life as a child, Elder L. Tom Perry said that his family members dressed each day not only in clothes that protected them from the physical storms but also in the armor of God. He went on to say that "as we would kneel in family prayer and listen to our father . . . pour out his soul to the Lord for the protection of his family against the fiery darts of the wicked, one more layer was added to our shield of faith" (see *Ensign*, May 1974, pp. 98–99).

The Lord has promised us that as we humble ourselves and call on his holy name and "watch and pray continually," we will "not be tempted above that which [we] can bear" (Alma 13:28). The Spirit of the Lord encourages us to pray, but because Satan understands the great protective power of prayer he tells us that we "must not pray" (2

Nephi 32:8). It is vital that we listen to the right Spirit, for prayer protects us against the power of the evil one. Without prayer, we cannot have this wonderful blessing of protection and peace.

Nephi gave us another good reason for praying. Talking about our church service, he taught that we "must not perform any thing unto the Lord save in the first place [we] shall pray unto the Father in the name of Christ, that he will consecrate [our] performance unto [us], that [our] performance may be for the welfare of [our] soul" (2 Nephi 32:9). What a wonderful promise! As we do our home teaching and visiting teaching and serve in our other Church responsibilities, we can receive the guidance we need to help others and experience significant soul growth ourselves.

Elder Bruce R. McConkie taught a third reason for praying: "There is nothing in the gospel that is better designed to keep the attention of men centered on God, on righteousness, and on their duties than is prayer. Every thought, word, and act is influenced or governed by the nature and extent of one's communion through prayer with Deity." (*Mormon Doctrine* [Salt Lake City: Bookcraft, 1966], p. 581.)

In the busy world we live in, it is so easy to get caught up in things of lesser importance and forget the covenants we have made with our Heavenly Father. The act of praying morning and night, offering prayers over our meals, and praying as a family helps us remain focused on the things that are most precious to us—our family, our membership in God's church, and our opportunity to gain eternal life. This constant reminder is exceedingly significant in our quest for exaltation.

A fourth reason for prayer was discussed by Elder David E. Sorensen. After teaching that prayer is more than just a way of obtaining blessings from God, he explained:

> Prayer itself is an act of faith as well as an act of righteousness. Prayer is the defining act of the worshipper of God the Father and his Son Jesus Christ. This is because the act of prayer itself can change and purify us, both individually and as a group. . . .
> While the blessings we ask for and receive through prayer are

undeniably magnificent, the greatest blessing and benefit is not the physical or spiritual blessings that may come as answers to our prayers but in the changes to our soul that come as we learn to be dependent on our Heavenly Father for strength. . . .

. . . As we humble ourselves to approach our God and thoughtfully consider His grace and great love for us, we will become a more holy and reverent people, more able to receive the blessings He will willingly pour out on us. *(Ensign*, May 1993, pp. 30–31.)

Improving Our Prayers

Speaking with God is a sacred opportunity, and sometimes we fail to give our prayers the preparation and thought that our Father in Heaven deserves. Here are some suggestions that may be helpful as we strive to communicate better with him.

1. *Precede prayer with contemplation and meditation.* Given the choice, most of us would never present a talk in church or give a business presentation without preparing beforehand. How much more important it is to think through what we want to say to God. Yet many times we may approach Heavenly Father with little, if any, preparation for doing so. We should pray according to our current situation and needs. For example, a sacrament meeting invocation would differ from that meeting's benediction, and a home evening prayer would differ from a personal prayer. We should include the Lord in our preparation so the Spirit can guide our thoughts and feelings into areas that we might never consider on our own.

This preparatory contemplation consists of much more than just five or ten minutes immediately before the prayer during which we think about what we want to say. Rather, we should pray continuously, as Amulek suggested in Alma 34:39. This continuous prayer can be seen as a form of meditation or pondering wherein our need for our Father in Heaven is seldom far from our heart and we consider our blessings and needs often throughout the day. This is opposite of being so caught up in the things of the world that we seldom consider God until it is time for our formal evening prayers—if we then remember them!

When we are striving to be humble and live the gospel, things that happen during the day will trigger thoughts of appreciation or desires for help from the Lord. For example, we might be playing with our children when our heart is suddenly filled with gratitude that God would allow us to be their earthly parents. We might at the same time recognize how much help we need to teach and rear them properly. These feelings will become some of the things that we mention in our evening prayers. The realization that we will soon be kneeling before God should cause us to constantly consider what we will discuss with him. Not only do these moments of meditation lead to more effective formal prayers, but also they are a form of prayer in and of themselves.

2. *During prayer, remain focused and confide in the Lord.* Elder H. Burke Peterson suggested the following process that can help all of us improve our prayers (see *Ensign,* January 1974, p. 19).

A. Go where you can be alone. Go where you can think. Go where you can kneel. Go where you can speak out loud to him. The bedroom, the bathroom, or the closet will do.

B. Now picture Heavenly Father in your mind's eye. Think of whom you are addressing. Control your thoughts—don't let them wander. Address him as your Father and your friend.

C. Now tell him things you really feel to tell him—avoid trite phrases that have little meaning. Have a sincere, heartfelt conversation with him. Confide in him, ask him for forgiveness, plead with him, enjoy him, thank him, express your love to him, and then listen for his answers. Listening is an essential part of praying.

This type of open, sincere communication with God was learned one day by a young German girl named Carla near the end of World War II. She was alone, playing the organ in a wartorn building that the Church used as a chapel in Hamburg. She was practicing the hymn "Nearer My God to Thee" when a loud knock came on the outside door. When she opened the door, she saw a young soldier in combat uniform. He said, "Excuse me, please. I heard an organ being played. I am Lieutenant Schwartz—I mean Brother Hans Schwartz—from Vienna." He held out his hand and asked, "You are a Latter-day Saint, aren't you?"

He explained that while he stood on the platform as his regiment was changing trains at the railroad station, he heard a beautiful, familiar hymn. When he followed the sound, he had been led to this particular building. Carla knew that the hand of God was involved, for the city was very noisy and the train station was three blocks away.

The soldier went on to explain that he had less than an hour before he had to leave again. He told how much he needed to pray and asked Carla if she would pray with him. She was stunned by the invitation and needed a little time to think, so she sat down at the organ and began to play the familiar tune again.

As she tried to get up enough courage to pray with him, the young man began to sing the hymn in a beautiful tenor voice. He moved onto the bench with Carla, and, as they sang through all the verses, her reservations about praying with him melted away.

The young man quietly told Carla that he knew he was going to die soon on the battlefield and asked her to kneel with him at the organ bench. He poured out his heart to God, telling him how much he loved him and what the gospel meant to him. He told him that he wanted to live so very much so he could be a teacher of truth and right, yet said that if it were the Lord's will, he was willing to die.

By the time the young soldier finished praying, Carla's eyes were heavy with tears and she had completely forgotten that this man was a stranger. It was easy for her to lay her whole heart open as he did, and, as she did so, she could feel the presence of heavenly beings.

Carla said that when their prayer was over, the young man reached for her hand and said, "God bless you, sister. It will all be much easier now." Though Carla has never seen this young man again, she knows that wherever he is, he is close to God. (See Carla Sansom, *Improvement Era*, July 1970, p. 19.)

As this young soldier prayed openly to his Heavenly Father, Carla learned a great lesson that has increased her effectiveness in praying. We can model this same principle for our families by becoming more specific in our prayers. For example, instead of saying" Bless each of us with the Spirit today," we can think of specific areas of help that are needed, such as, "Sally is struggling to help her friend understand the gospel better. Please guide her thoughts and actions as she studies and strives to help her friend come closer to thee." Most of our prayers need this added intimacy, this open frank conversation with God. We don't go up to our friends, tell them that we need help, and let it go at that. We tell them what help we need. We do the same thing when it comes to gratitude. Much more appreciated than just "thanks for everything" is a statement that reminds us of some specific things we have done that our friend has appreciated. This is the way we should talk with God. More than "Bless our son in the mission field," or "Thank you for the blessings thou dost give us," we should share with our Father some of the concerns we have for our son and some of the things we are most grateful for. When we open our hearts to him, like Carla and the young soldier, we will feel the presence of heavenly beings.

Recognizing Answers to Our Prayers

We live in a loud, noisy world, and the Holy Ghost speaks in a still, small voice. Despite the seeming quietness of that voice, it will penetrate deep into our hearts if we will but find ways to filter out some of the noise and distraction of the world. Talking about the difficulty of listening in today's world, Elder Graham W. Doxey said:

> *Time* to listen. The *ability* to listen. The *desire* to listen. On religious matters, too many of us are saying, "What did you say? Speak up; I can't hear you." And when he doesn't *shout* back, or cause the bush to burn, or write us a message in stone with his finger, we are inclined to think he doesn't listen, doesn't care about us. Some even conclude there is no God. . . .
>
> The questions are not, "Does God live? Does God love me? Does God speak to me?" The critical question is, "Are you listening to him?" . . . It is the same for *you* as it was for Elijah, as it is with the modern-day prophets: "The still, small voice is still small." (*Ensign*, November 1991, p. 25.)

Elder Doxey then explained three "aids to our hearing" that are available to each of us. His first aid is to revitalize our weekly worship. We should do more than just sing the hymns, we should ponder the meaning of the words, enjoy the spirit of the music, and sing with enthusiasm. He pointed out the importance of partaking of the sacrament, not merely taking the sacrament. This is done by sincerely recommitting ourselves to keep the commandments and do the will of the Lord. This will allow the Spirit of the Lord to be with us and guide us.

His second aid to hearing is to pray to know God's will, not to "get things" from the Lord. Sometimes we have to give up the things that we think will make us happy in order to receive from the Lord the things that really bring true peace and joy. Elder Doxey used as an example the hundreds of missionary couples who are needed in the mission field, but they must first give up their firm grip on the familiarities of home and of children and grandchildren. The Lord is prepared to perform miracles in their behalf, but they refuse to follow his counsel and instead ask for things that they feel they need. When we can truly pray with the attitude of "not my will but Thy will be done," we will be sufficiently contrite to receive God's inspiration and guidance.

His third suggestion for better hearing the word of the Lord has to do with the scriptures. The Lord has told us that he speaks through the scriptures. As we study the scriptures each day, we need to search for answers and listen to what the scriptures and the Spirit are telling us.

Remember that answers to prayers usually come quietly—a burning in the bosom, the voice of the Lord coming into our minds, a quiet assurance that some course of action is right. The most often-mentioned method in the scriptures is that of enlightening our minds, speaking peace to our minds, and filling our souls with joy (see D&C 6:15, 23; 8:2; 11:13–14). The Lord will speak to us in ways that will be most effective for us. It is our responsibility to learn to recognize how we feel when the Spirit is communicating with us.

It is also important to remember that answers to prayers are dependent on more than just prayer. As you read the following statement by Elder Neal A. Maxwell, identify the three things that affect answers to our prayers.

> Petitioning in prayer has taught me, again and again, that the vault of heaven with all its blessings is to be opened only by a combination lock. One tumbler falls when there is faith, a second when there is per-

sonal righteousness; the third and final tumbler falls only when what is sought is, in God's judgment—not ours—right for us. Sometimes we pound on the vault door for something we want very much and wonder why the door does not open. We would be very spoiled children if that vault door opened any more easily than it does. I can tell, looking back, that God truly loves me by inventorying the petitions He has refused to grant me. (*New Era*, April 1978, p. 6.)

Answers to prayers do not always come easily. Even great spiritual men like President Marion G. Romney stated: "There have been times in my life when it was very difficult for me to get through to the Lord and when I've had to fast and pray for periods each week over long months of time. But it can be done." (*Improvement Era*, April 1966, p. 301.) It would be a serious mistake to assume that every prayer will be answered immediately. Some prayers take considerable time and effort on our part. God loves us and will give us the direction we need, but this direction will be according to his timetable, not ours. He expects us to seek his will and then to act the best we can. He will not allow us to go too far wrong before we begin to receive negative or uneasy feelings, but he is trying to help us develop wisdom and judgment and to become more like him. We would not grow if he automatically solved all our problems and gave us all the answers. When he withholds an answer from us, we can be assured that it is because of his great love for us. He understands us and our abilities. He knows what is best for us and wants us to gain the experience that will help in the growth of the soul.

Prayer Language

In this life we show respect to others by addressing them in formal ways such as Elder, Bishop, Judge, and President. This same concept should carry over to the language we use in prayers. We are taught that we should lay aside our everyday language when we pray and use the language that is found in the scriptures. Elder Dallin H. Oaks discussed this special language of prayer and encouraged us to become familiar with it.

In our day the English words *thee*, *thou*, *thy*, and *thine* are suitable for the language of prayer, not because of how they were used anciently but because they are currently obsolete in common English discourse. Being unused in everyday communications, they are now available as a distinctive form of address in English, appropriate to symbolize respect, closeness, and reverence for the one being addressed. . . .

Men and women who wish to show respect will take the time to learn the special language of prayer. Persons spend many hours mastering communication skills in other mediums, such as poetry or prose, vocal or instrumental music, and even the language of access to computers. My brothers and sisters, the manner of addressing our Heavenly Father in prayer is at least as important as these. (*Ensign*, May 1993, pp. 17–18.)

One of the best ways to become more comfortable with the language of prayer is through daily scripture study. The scriptures model how these special words should be used; through our frequent study, these words become second nature with us. As we use these words in our prayers, we help our children and others assimilate this reverent and loving language in their prayers.

Continual Prayer

In Alma 34:39, Amulek tells us that we need to be "watchful unto prayer continually" in order to avoid the temptations of the devil. In the same chapter Amulek tells us that we should pray when we are in our fields, our homes, and the wilderness. He goes on to say that when we are not involved in formal prayer, we should "let [our] hearts be full, drawn out in prayer unto him continually for [our] welfare, and also for the welfare of those who are around [us]." (See Alma 34:18–27.)

Sister Patricia P. Pinegar of the Young Women general presidency told of an experience she had when she was seventeen that helped her focus on the Lord throughout the day:

My friends and I went to a fireside where the speaker taught us about our Savior's love. . . .

The speaker suggested that to help us remember to think about the Savior, we could listen to the school bell that rang often during the day. Each time we heard the bell, we were to say a silent prayer, even with our eyes open, even walking down the hall. . . . He taught us that in just a few seconds, many times during the day, we could practice thinking about our Heavenly Father and Savior. . . .

He also warned us that all of this might seem awkward at first but that if we chose to try, we could truly be filled with His love, our faith really would grow, and we would feel joy.

That sounded wonderful to me. I decided to try. I could not believe how many times the bell rang each day. When I heard it, I stopped. "Heavenly Father, thank you. Please bless me and bless Dorene. I know she's having struggles." It was awkward at first, but soon I found myself thinking about my Heavenly Father and Savior, not only when the bell rang but many times during the day. . . . My faith had increased and I was happy. (*Ensign*, May 1994, p. 94.)

Prayer is much more than words. Prayer includes the love and devotion that come from deep within our hearts. The yearning that we have to live the gospel, the gratitude we feel for the numerous blessings we enjoy, and our deep-felt need for the Lord's help all constitute a silent but constant prayer unto God.

If we find ourselves losing touch with God during the day, we can do as Sister Pinegar did and choose something to remind us until constant prayer becomes a way of life with us. This may be no more than setting our clock or wrist watch to buzz at regular intervals during the day. Then we will be able to testify, along with Sister Pinegar, that our love for God has increased, that the help we receive from God has greatly multiplied, and that we enjoy happiness that we never realized was possible.

Chapter Twelve

THE LORD'S
PRINCIPLES OF WAR
Alma 43–62

Introduction

In 1967 Elder Marion G. Romney observed that "Informed Latter-day Saints know that this earth will never again, during its telestial existence, be free from civil disturbance and war" (*Improvement Era*, June 1967, p. 77). This is one reason why the Book of Mormon is so helpful to us today. The principles it teaches concerning war give us the guidance we need in order to make the correct decisions in our tumultuous modern world.

As Latter-day Saints, it is our duty to do everything we can do to renounce war and proclaim peace. The Church is against war, but there are times when, as citizens of our individual countries, we have a responsibility to protect our freedoms and our loved ones. The Book of Mormon can help us understand and develop the proper attitudes concerning war.

Anger and Hate

Anger, hate, and revenge are never acceptable reasons for war. These feelings come from the devil (see 3 Nephi 11:29) and effectively block all attempts at solving problems peacefully. Not only do these feelings drive away the Holy Ghost, which is the only true source of peace, but they also cloud our ability to reason and they place us in a position where we can be easily manipulated.

This is brought out very clearly in Alma 43, which tells of a Lamanite attack on the Nephite people. Men of the Amalekites and the Zoramites, two groups of Nephite apostates who had joined the Lamanites, were appointed as chief captains over the Lamanites because they had a more wicked and murderous disposition than the Lamanites. These leaders were to stir up Lamanite anger and hatred against the Nephites so that they could get these Lamanites to fight the Nephites and thus gain great power over them (see Alma 43:5–8).

This principle, as do most of the principles of war, carry over into our personal relationships with others. When we allow our hearts to be filled with anger or hate, we lose the promptings of the Holy Ghost and place ourselves in the power of Satan or those who follow him. When these feelings come to us, we need to ponder and pray through them before we do things that we will later regret.

Justifiable Reasons for War

At no time in the Book of Mormon were the righteous armies the aggressors, nor did they make preemptive attacks against an enemy that was obviously about to launch a war. They never waged wars of national interest where any issue but immediate survival was at stake, and they never killed or mistreated prisoners.

When our purposes for war are righteous ones, I believe the Lord will help us. The following verses mention several justifiable reasons for going to war.

> . . . They were not fighting for monarchy nor power but they were fighting for their homes and their liberties, their wives and their children, and their all, yea, for their rites of worship and their church.
>
> And they were doing that which they felt was the duty which they owed to their God; for the Lord had said unto them, and also unto their fathers, that: Inasmuch as ye are not guilty of the first offense, neither

the second, ye shall not suffer yourselves to be slain by the hands of your enemies.

And again, the Lord has said that: Ye shall defend your families even unto bloodshed. Therefore for this cause were the Nephites contending with the Lamanites, to defend themselves, and their families, and their lands, their country, and their rights, and their religion. (Alma 43:45–47.)

Proper Attitudes toward War

The book of Alma contains many examples of righteous attitudes toward war. When the Nephite army was righteous and entered war with the following five attitudes, they fought "in the strength of the Lord." Otherwise they were "weak like unto [their enemy]." (See Mormon 2:26.)

1. *The Nephites went to war reluctantly.* The Nephites were "compelled reluctantly to contend with their brethren," and "their wars never did cease for the space of many years with the Lamanites, notwithstanding their much reluctance" (Alma 48:21–22).

The gospel teaches us that we should love our enemies and do everything we can do to make them our friends. We realize that until they become our friends our opportunity to share the gospel with them is limited, and we also realize that the gospel is the only source of lasting peace. Until men and women have peace in their hearts, there will never be peace in the world. The last thing we should ever want to do is go to war as a nation or contend as an individual out of hostility and aggression.

2. *Their only desire was to defend themselves.* The Lamanites' intention was to "destroy their brethren, or to subject them and bring them into bondage." The Nephites' only desire was to be left alone to "preserve their lands, and their liberty, and their church" (Alma 43:29–30). Moroni pointed out that, because the Nephite reasons for going to war were righteous, and because of their religion and faith, the Lord would help them (see Alma 44:3).

3. *They disliked the shedding of blood.* The Nephites were "sorry to take up arms against the Lamanites, because they did not delight in

the shedding of blood." These people loved the Lamanites even if their love was not reciprocated, and they felt "sorry to be the means of sending so many of their brethren out of this world . . . unprepared to meet their God." They went to war because they felt they had no choice, for they could not permit "that their wives and their children should be massacred by the barbarous cruelty of those who were once their brethren." (Alma 48:23–24.)

The attitude we have toward the shedding of blood determines whether we murder when we take someone's life during war. If we only shed blood when we have to and if we abhor doing so, it is not considered murder and we are still clean before God. This attitude is demonstrated in the following story.

Peter Nolte was a young lieutenant in the German army during World War II. Following the war he moved with his family to Albuquerque, New Mexico, and started a business repairing foreign cars. Peter shared an experience that took place during the Battle of the Bulge.

In that German offensive it was hard to know exactly where the line of battle was from one day to the next. I was ordered one morning to take my men into a small German village. We were to secure a bridge on its outskirts. As we left the town and approached the bridge, I saw a U.S. Army jeep parked in the middle of the bridge. An American soldier was sitting with his back to us behind the steering wheel. I quietly walked up to him, and in my best English I informed him that my men and I had come to secure the bridge and if he valued his life he had better make a run for it. He looked at me and then at my men. Without saying anything he jumped out of the jeep, ran across the bridge, and disappeared into the trees.

He left the jeep right there. The keys were still in it. My men and I had never seen an American automobile before. We took turns driving it around town and back and forth across the bridge until it ran out of gas. . . .

But there is more to this story. About five years ago a man brought his car into my shop in Albuquerque. It needed some rather major repairs. When he came to pick it up, I gave him the work order which broke down the man hours and parts on the repair job. When he handed

me his check, he said, "I know you. You saved my life on a bridge outside of a German town in the last war!"

I couldn't believe it, but he was right. We had met before. We are
good friends now. We even play golf together now and then. (Jim Kimball, "Traveling Light" column in the *Deseret News*, date unknown.)

A soldier who did not respect life may very well have considered
the man on the bridge an enemy and taken his life. In this case, Peter
would have killed not only a child of God but also a future customer
and friend.

4. *The Nephites desired to stop the bloodshed as soon as possible.*
During one major battle, even though they were outnumbered by more
than two to one, the Nephites managed to encircle the Lamanite army.
When the Lamanites realized they were surrounded, their hearts were
filled with terror. As soon as Moroni saw the terror of the Lamanites,
he commanded his soldiers to stop shedding their blood.

Moroni approached Zerahemnah, the Lamanite leader, and told
him that they had no desire to slay him and his men. He told Zerahemnah that he would allow all of the Lamanites to go free if they
would give their word that they would not attack the Nephite people
again. When Zerahemnah refused to make this promise, the battle
resumed. However, when he saw that his army would be completely
destroyed, Zerahemnah cried out to Moroni. Moroni again stopped the
battle. After making a covenant of peace, the Lamanites were allowed
to depart into the wilderness. This ended that conflict between the
Lamanites and the Nephites (see Alma 44:19–24).

Moroni and his army could have destroyed all the enemy soldiers,
but, because they abhorred bloodshed, they stopped the conflict as
soon as they possibly could. Numerous lives on both sides of the
battle were saved because of this attitude, and the Lord continued to
bless the Nephite armies because of their righteousness.

In the heat of battle we sometimes forget that the enemy soldiers
are also sons and daughters of God. A soldier during the Vietnam War
found himself becoming more and more callous toward the shedding
of blood until he came in possession of a diary taken off a dead enemy
soldier. That night, by the light of a small cooking fire, he read from a
rough translation the last recorded thoughts of his so-called enemy:

I do not know where we are. Our officers say that we are fighting bravely against American imperialists who have invaded our homeland. We fight bravely, but we are poorly supplied. I am lonely. I miss my family far away. I wonder how they are doing. I miss my home and wish to be back in the mountains and walk in the forests. I wish to see again the flowers, the birds, and animals of home.

The soldier was stunned by what he read. He realized that these were not the words of an enemy but of someone who under different circumstances could have been a friend. Suddenly he understood that the North Vietnamese people were not the real enemy; the enemy was Satan and the evil that he waged on the hearts of mankind. Stephen concluded his story with the following insight:

That day in Vietnam, as I sat by the fire, I discovered that happiness comes from understanding the worth of a human soul regardless of race, creed, or political views, and from knowing that we are all children of our Father in Heaven. To know this is to love all people, even those who may appear to be the enemy. (Stephen G. Biddulph, *Ensign,* January 1994, pp. 63–64.)

5. *Wars can be won by faith and righteousness more effectively than by huge arms races.* Captain Moroni taught of the value of faith and righteousness when he stated: "Ye see that God will support, and keep, and preserve us, so long as we are faithful unto him, and unto our faith, and our religion; and never will the Lord suffer that we shall be destroyed except we should fall into transgression and deny our faith" (Alma 44:4). Even though the Nephites were greatly outnumbered at this time, they won the war because of their faith and obedience.

Talking about our day, President Spencer W. Kimball said:

O foolish men who think to protect the world with armaments, battleships, and space equipment, when only righteousness is needed!

. . . We depend on fortifications, or gods of stone; upon ships and planes and projectiles, our gods of iron—gods which have no ears, no eyes, no hearts. We pray to them for deliverance and depend upon them for protection . . . like the gods of Baal. (*The Teachings of Spencer W. Kimball* [Salt Lake City: Bookcraft, 1982], p. 416.)

We are a warlike people, easily distracted from our assignment of preparing for the coming of the Lord. . . . When threatened, we become antienemy instead of pro-kingdom of God. (P. 417.)

God will fight our battles if we honor him and serve him with all our hearts, might, mind, and strength (p. 416).

When to Fight and When Not to Fight

The following examples from the Book of Mormon show times when the people were to go to war and times when they were to refuse to fight.

Example One (see Mosiah 23–24). Alma and others who had accepted the gospel had to flee into the wilderness in order to protect their lives. They came to a beautiful land and soon began to prosper exceedingly. They built a fine city named Helam.

One day while Alma's people were working in their fields, they saw a Lamanite army approaching. They fled to the city, where they asked Alma what they should do. He told them not to be frightened and promised them that if they remembered the Lord He would eventually deliver them. They immediately began to cry to the Lord that he would soften the hearts of the Lamanites so that they would be spared.

As the army approached, Alma and his people delivered themselves into the hands of the Lamanites, and the Lord did soften their hearts so that they did not kill the people of Alma. In this instance God did not want his people to fight. He later helped these people to escape and join the other Nephites in the land of Zarahemla.

Example Two (see Alma 24). The Lamanites who were converted by the sons of Mosiah in several different cities and lands called themselves Anti-Nephi-Lehies. The Lamanites who had not joined the Church became angry and took up arms against the converted Lamanites. When the Anti-Nephi-Lehies heard that the Lamanites were preparing to destroy them, they refused to take up arms in their defense. Their king explained their feelings in the following words:

I thank my God, my beloved people, that our great God has in goodness sent these our brethren, the Nephites, unto us to preach unto us, and to convince us of the traditions of our wicked fathers.

And behold, I thank my great God that he has given us a portion of his Spirit to soften our hearts. . . .

And behold, I also thank my God, that . . . we have been convinced of our sins, and of the many murders which we have committed.

And I also thank my God . . . that he hath granted unto us that we might repent of these things, and also that he hath forgiven us of those our many sins and murders which we have committed, and taken away the guilt from our hearts, through the merits of his Son.

And now behold, my brethren, since it has been all that we could do . . . to repent of all our sins and the many murders which we have committed, . . . let us stain our swords no more with the blood of our brethren. (Alma 24:7–12.)

Once these people had been brought to the truth they "would suffer even unto death rather than commit sin" (Alma 24:19). To make sure that they did not shed further blood, they buried their weapons deep in the earth and covenanted that they would never again shed man's blood. As the Lamanite army approached, the Anti-Nephi-Lehies went out to meet them, prostrated themselves upon the ground, and began to call upon the Lord in prayer. While they were praying, the Lamanite army came upon them and killed a thousand and five of them.

When the Lamanites saw that their brethren would not flee or fight and that, in the very act of perishing, they praised God, many of their hearts were touched, and more than a thousand Lamanites joined the people of God. Many souls were saved because the people of God did what the Lord wanted them to do in this instance and refused to fight.

Example Three. In Alma 51 we read about a group of people who desired to change the government and establish a king. Those who supported this movement were called kingmen, and they caused a great contention in the land. The problem was settled when a majority of the people voted against the kingmen.

About this time the Nephites learned that the Lamanites were again preparing to come against them in battle. When the kingmen heard this, they were glad in their hearts and refused to take up arms to defend their country. This caused a serious problem, for the Nephites needed to be united in order to maintain their freedom.

Under the direction of Moroni, a Nephite army marched against the kingmen. Four thousand kingmen were killed, their leaders were cast into prison, and the remainder of the kingmen joined the Nephites in protecting their country. In this particular situation, the right thing to do was to go to war to defend their country.

The Effects of War

Because we read so much about the negative impact that war has on many soldiers, we may overlook the fact that numerous other soldiers actually strengthen their relationship with God. Mormon points out that "many had become hardened, because of the exceedingly great length of the war; and many were softened because of their afflictions, insomuch that they did humble themselves before God, even in the depth of humility" (Alma 62:41). Whether a person becomes more hardened or more spiritual is greatly dependent on his attitude towards the war. Here are two stories that illustrate the blessings that can come to those who stay close to the Lord. The first story is told by a Latter-day Saint German who served his country during World War II.

In World War II, I was a soldier for my country for five years. For a time, I was in charge of guarding Russian prisoners. These prisoners had to work very hard. I remember one man in particular—a teacher who was able to speak a little German. I tried to help him as much as possible in my position. I remembered the words of the Savior that we should love our enemies. The teacher and others I had command over showed me their thankfulness by trusting in me and by calling me their father. A short time later, I was transferred to the Russian front where a few of us were captured and put into a Soviet prison. We were sentenced to be shot the next day.

A soldier came to bring us out of prison and take us to a bunker, where we were to be guarded until our execution. To my surprise, the soldier was the teacher—the same man I had befriended a short time before when we were in quite the opposite position. . . . He recognized me and said, "You, good man, helped us—now I will help you, too!"

He came to us in the night and let us out of the bunker. He took us to an area close to a German encampment and let us go free. My life was spared, I believe, because I had tried to follow the words of the Savior. (Taken from his grandfather's journal by Bruce Crandall, *Ensign*, March 1994, p. 28.)

The second story deals with the same man. He and a hundred other soldiers found themselves surrounded by the enemy and facing certain capture. The group was led by a young, inexperienced officer who asked this man if he knew of any way out of their situation. The man answered that he did but only the Lord could provide it. When he received permission from his officer to go ahead, he assembled the men in a short service in which they sang a hymn and he quoted a scripture. They then prayed for guidance and deliverance. As they finished their prayer, a dense fog rolled in and completely covered their surroundings, which allowed them to escape without detection. (Ibid., p. 29.)

Captain Moroni, the stripling warriors, Mormon and his son Moroni—all these illustrate that great righteousness can be maintained in the midst of war. By following the principles that these great men taught and lived, we will be able to stay close to the Lord during those times that we face aggression in our lives.

Chapter Thirteen

ONE BY ONE
3 Nephi 11, 17

Introduction

A stake president and other Church leaders visited a class of young children. The teacher welcomed them and then, desiring to impress on the children the importance of the priesthood leaders, asked a class member, "How many important people are here today?"

The child stood up and began counting out loud until she reached the total of seventeen. The child had included every person in the room—both the visitors and the children.

After telling this story in general conference, Elder Marion D. Hanks concluded by saying, "That is how Christ feels, and so should we." (See *Ensign*, January 1973, p. 127.)

President Spencer W. Kimball demonstrated this same sensitivity for the value of each person while participating in an area conference in the Dominican Republic. Sixteen hundred members of the Church had already attended the evening conference session and President and Sister Kimball were now asleep in their room when a knock came on their door. His secretary apologized for disturbing him and told him of a hundred people who had just arrived. They had jammed themselves into one bus and driven all day so they could attend the conference session. After such a great effort, they had experienced engine trouble and had arrived one hour after the conference had concluded.

The secretary thought that President Kimball might like to dictate a message that could be shared with them, but this was not good enough for President Kimball. He got dressed and went downstairs, where he found these weary travelers weeping because they had missed the opportunity of listening to a prophet of God.

President Kimball spent over an hour visiting with them, helping them feel relieved and satisfied that their trip had been indeed worthwhile. They then got back on the bus for the long ride home so they could be at work and school the next morning. As President Kimball returned to his bed, he did so with peace and contentment in his soul. (See Spencer W. Kimball, *Ensign*, May 1981, pp. 45–46.)

The Importance of Each Individual

Throughout his ministry Jesus did many things that show us the value of each individual. Consider, for example, his desire to share living water with the Samaritan woman at the well, his willingness and even eagerness to bless and associate with groups of children even though his Apostles were ready to turn them away, and his concern for his mother and for the thief while he hung on the cross.

Nowhere is his love for each person better demonstrated than during his appearance to the Nephite people. When we realize that there were approximately twenty-five hundred Nephites that he ministered to, his concern for the one becomes even more powerful and enlightening. After Jesus had introduced himself and the people had fallen to the earth, he spoke to them, saying:

> Arise and come forth unto me, that ye may thrust your hands into my side, and also that ye may feel the prints of the nails in my hands and in my feet, that ye may know that I am the God of Israel, and the God of the whole earth, and have been slain for the sins of the world.
>
> And it came to pass that the multitude went forth, and thrust their hands into his side, and did feel the prints of the nails in his hands and in his feet; and this they did do, going forth one by one until they had all gone forth, and did see with their eyes and did feel with their hands, and

did know of a surety and did bear record, that it was he, of whom it was written by the prophets, that should come. (3 Nephi 11:14–15.)

For twenty-five hundred people to quietly and reverently approach the Savior and personally make both physical and spiritual contact with him must have taken a considerable amount of time, yet the Savior wanted each of them to experience this special blessing.

After calling the Nephite Twelve and teaching the people many things, Jesus said that he would leave them and return again the next day. But as he looked around at the people, he could tell that they did not want him to leave and he was filled with compassion. He then said:

> Have ye any that are sick among you? Bring them hither. Have ye any that are lame, or blind, or halt, or maimed, or leprous, or that are withered, or that are deaf, or that are afflicted in any manner? Bring them hither and I will heal them, for I have compassion upon you; my bowels are filled with mercy.
>
> For I perceive that ye desire that I should show unto you what I have done unto your brethren at Jerusalem, for I see that your faith is sufficient that I should heal you.
>
> And it came to pass that when he had thus spoken, all the multitude, with one accord, did go forth with their sick and their afflicted, and their lame, and with their blind, and with their dumb, and with all them that were afflicted in any manner; and he did heal them every one as they were brought forth unto him. (3 Nephi 17:7–9.)

Later that same day, Jesus "took their little children, one by one, and blessed them, and prayed unto the Father for them. And when he had done this he wept again" because of his joy. (3 Nephi 17:21–22.)

Jesus could have healed the people and blessed the children as a group, but by taking the time to bless each one individually he revealed how deeply he was concerned for each individual person and taught us the importance of reaching out to the one. Later Jesus referred to these events and said, "Ye see that I have commanded that none of you should go away, but rather have commanded that ye should come unto me, that ye might feel and see; even so shall ye do unto the world" (3 Nephi 18:25).

This same concern for the one is taught in the following story, which was told to me by a temple president. While serving a mission for the Church a young sister missionary whom we'll call Joan contracted polio, and her parents had to bring her home in an iron lung. The family adjusted to the fact that she would spend the rest of her life in the iron lung.

The bishop assigned ward members to help care for Joan. They would massage her muscles, apply lotion to her skin, visit with her, and do other things that would add to her comfort. Many times people who were discouraged were deliberately chosen to assist Joan, for the bishop found that they soon began to appreciate the many blessings they had been overlooking. He asked a couple to help Joan who had been bitter for many years. Their son and grandson had been killed in a wreck, and they had become bitter and inactive. They had quit working in the temple and had refused to have anything to do with the Church, but they did accept the invitation to help Joan.

As they worked with Joan, their hearts began to soften. One day Joan mentioned that, even though she knew it wasn't possible, she often wished she could return to the temple again. This couple contacted the temple president and asked him if there was anything that could be done to fulfill Joan's wish. The president was doubtful but promised that he would discuss it with his staff. To his surprise, his staff were really excited and thought they could do it. (This was a temple where the patrons had to move from room to room during the endowment.) Even the electrician was positive it could be done and, when they found that a 220-volt electrical power source was needed to run the iron lung, they rewired the rooms to meet that need.

Finally the wonderful day came when Joan was able to visit the temple again. She was accompanied by 150 friends and relatives, including the couple who had overcome their bitterness and become active in the Church again.

Every one of us is precious and valuable in the sight of God. And every person in turn should be of great worth to each of us. As we concentrate less on the group and more on each member of that group, our service becomes more rewarding and we become more like the Savior.

Our Inner Potential

A woman once asked Elder Sterling W. Sill if he had ever seen God. He gave the following insightful response: "I have not seen Him since the day of my birth on March 31, 1903. But I saw Him many times prior to that time." (*Ensign*, June 1987, p. 34.) God knows us well. He lived with us for innumerable years in our premortal life, and he knows well our individual and collective potential. As we listen to the whisperings of his Spirit, we can help ourselves and others better fulfill our divine potential. This inspiring truth was learned by Ned Combs as he was serving as a second counselor in a bishopric. He had struggled to determine which deacon he should recommend to the bishop to be called as the new deacons quorum president.

He finally narrowed the possibilities to three worthy thirteen-year-olds, but he was unable to receive the confirmation that he desired from the Lord. As he went over the list of deacons again, his attention became centered on a young man named Kevin. He had skipped over him the previous time because Kevin was deaf. As he pondered some of the difficulties Kevin might face in such a calling, he realized that Kevin needed the calling in order to develop his ability to express himself and improve his leadership abilities. As he prayed about this choice, he received a strong assurance that the call should be made.

This was the beginning of seven wonderful years of growth for Kevin. "He learned effective leadership—he delegated authority, gave talks, helped with service projects, and blessed the sacrament. He became a tremendous influence for good among the youth."

One evening, Kevin stopped by Ned's home and showed him the mission call he had just received from President Spencer W. Kimball. He was thrilled to be able to serve and had received the assurance that the call had come from his Father in Heaven. Later, at the airport, with tears streaming down his smiling face and his voice quivering, Kevin thanked Ned for what he had done for him. Ned learned that day that most of us are, "only as handicapped as we allow ourselves to be." (Ned B. Combs, *Ensign*, February 1980, p. 63.)

Ned overlooked Kevin's tremendous potential until the Lord

helped him see what could happen in Kevin's life. Because the Lord recognizes our potential, he will call us to positions that will allow us to develop this potential—if we will prepare ourselves and be willing to accept his calls.

Spiritual Growth—One Person at a Time

Sometimes when we are called to teach a class, we forget that we are not teaching a class, but a classroom filled with individuals. Each student assimilates at his or her own level and rate the things we are teaching. Faith may grow in one heart this week and in someone else's heart the next.

Home teaching and visiting teaching are not made up of routes but of individual families who have different needs and wants. As we focus our attention on these families, lives are touched and testimonies grow. This concept of teaching the one was forcefully taught by Sister Jayne B. Malan, first counselor in the Young Women general presidency. When she was young, she and her sister were given the task of trying to feed 350 lambs that had lost their mothers. They were to save as many as they possibly could.

They tried numerous ways of feeding the lambs as a group, but none of them worked. They found that the only way that worked was to pick each lamb up in their arms and feed them like babies.

Every morning they would find several lambs that had died during the night. Some were killed by coyotes, but others starved to death while "surrounded by food they couldn't or wouldn't eat." One morning, when she found her favorite lamb lying dead under the willows, she gathered the lamb up in her arms and sought out her father. With tears streaming down her cheeks she asked him, "Dad, isn't there someone who can help us feed our lambs?"

After some thought, her father replied, "Jayne, once a long, long time ago, someone else said almost those same words. He said, 'Feed my lambs. . . . Feed my sheep. . . . Feed my sheep.'" (John 21:15–17.) (*Ensign,* November 1989, pp. 78–79.)

The Savior cares for many souls who need our help; like Sister Malan's lambs, many of them can only be fed one lamb at a time. As we help them realize how important they are to their Father in Heaven, they will begin to involve themselves in his church and kingdom. A good example of this was shared by Danel W. Bachman. While serving as full-time missionaries, he and his companion were teaching a family who was nearing baptism—except for their oldest daughter. She was a spiritual leader for the rest of the family, but something was holding her back.

On a regular fast Sunday, they fasted for this girl and met with the family after sacrament meeting. While Danel's companion was talking with the family, the Spirit revealed to Danel what was holding the daughter back from being baptized. Through the Spirit Danel further perceived that the Lord "knew her personally, understood her concern, and had great blessings ready to be poured out upon her."

Danel became so excited that he interrupted his companion and shared with the family what he had learned from the Holy Ghost. The next evening, when the elders returned with their zone leaders to interview the family for baptism, the girl asked if she could be interviewed also. The Spirit had borne witness to her of the things Danel had received the previous day. She was baptized along with her family. Once she realized how important she was to God, she was eager to do his will. (Danel W. Bachman, *Ensign*, March 1991, p. 41.)

God has given each of us everything we need to succeed. He knows our strengths and weaknesses and has a plan that will help us use our strengths and overcome our weaknesses. Each one of us is of precious worth to him, and he rejoices as we each make the decision to follow his gospel plan. Through the Holy Ghost he truly individualizes his gospel and feeds each of us one by one. He asks only that, as we come to know and understand the truths of the gospel, we make them available individually to those around us.

Chapter Fourteen

BECOMING
LIKE JESUS
3 Nephi 12 and Moroni 7

The Purpose of Earth Life

The purpose of this life is to become more like God so that eventually we will become gods ourselves. Jesus extended this invitation to us when he said, "What manner of men ought ye to be? Verily I say unto you, even as I am." (3 Nephi 27:27.) Joseph Smith taught, "If you wish to go where God is, you must be like God, or possess the principles which God possesses" (*Teachings of the Prophet Joseph Smith,* p. 216).

We realize that we will not become completely like God during this lifetime, but we can begin this journey and become much more like him than we are now. Elder Neal A. Maxwell explained this process when he stated: "As we accept Christ and become his children, there begins to be a change—even a 'mighty change' in us. As we earnestly strive to become one with him and his purposes, we come to resemble him." (*Brigham Young University 1989–90 Devotional and Fireside Speeches* (Provo, Utah: 1990), p. 87.)

The Christian writer C. S. Lewis perceived this concept:

> When [Jesus] said, "Be perfect" He meant it. He meant that we must

go in for the full treatment. It is hard; but the sort of compromise we are all hankering after is harder—in fact, it is impossible. It may be hard for an egg to turn into a bird: it would be a jolly sight harder for it to learn to fly while remaining an egg. We are like eggs at present. And you cannot go on indefinitely being just an ordinary, decent egg. We must be hatched or go bad. . . .

This is the whole of Christianity. There is nothing else. It is so easy to get muddled about that. . . . The Church exists for nothing else but to draw men into Christ, to make them little Christs. If they are not doing that, all the cathedrals, clergy, missions, sermons, even the Bible itself, are simply a waste of time. God became Man for no other purpose. It is even doubtful, you know, whether the whole universe was created for any other purpose. (*Mere Christianity* [New York: Macmillan, 1952], pp. 169–70.)

One danger in not seeing the major reason why we are here is that we might focus on things of lesser importance. For example, getting a body, keeping the commandments, and being tested are only means to an end, not the end itself. As we focus on becoming more like the Savior, we find ourselves approaching life differently. How we approach our meetings, serve in the Church, view the commandments, treat others, and feel about life all begin to change.

Our Motives Are Important

We did not come to this earth just to do but rather to become. Our purpose is not merely to do honest things but to become honest; not just to perform charitable acts but to become charitable. If our hearts are right and our motives pure, doing will lead to becoming. If we are not careful, we may fall into the trap of ritual obedience. We might go to church because that is what we believe good Mormons do, and not because we want to worship, learn, and make covenants with our Father in Heaven. Perhaps we do our home teaching or visiting teaching because our ward is striving for 100 percent teaching or because we have not missed for over three years or because our companion presses us to go. Such motivation may get us to attain high numbers, but it often does little to help us become like God. As we ponder the real purpose of home teaching or visiting teaching and then visit the families out of concern for their welfare, our love for them will deepen and our nature will become more Godlike. This same principle applies to every commandment that God has given us. Mormon discussed the importance of one's motives:

> For behold, God hath said a man being evil cannot do that which is good; for if he offereth a gift, or prayeth unto God, except he shall do it with real intent it profiteth him nothing. . . .
>
> And likewise also is it counted evil unto a man, if he shall pray and not with real intent of heart; yea, and it profiteth him nothing, for God receiveth none such.
>
> Wherefore, a man being evil cannot do that which is good; neither will he give a good gift.
>
> For behold, a bitter fountain cannot bring forth good water. (Moroni 7:6, 9–11.)

Why we serve is as important as how we serve; spiritual growth and divine direction occur most effectively when our hearts are right. When our purpose is to bless the lives of others and expand the kingdom of God, we are more receptive to the help and influence of the Holy Ghost and we become more like our Father in Heaven.

Motives may very well be the reason why some receive joy in their service and others do not. They may be why many feel the Spirit in a Church meeting while some just watch the clock. Proper motives make our prayers into real communication with God instead of just words that seem to go nowhere. Motives are the difference between true religious worship and just going through the motions.

To serve for the right reasons is to serve for the reasons that Christ served: this kind of service benefits both the giver and the receiver.

A Mighty Change of Heart

It takes more than rote obedience to change our basic nature and attitudes. We must understand what God's purposes are and then desire to help fulfill them. This mighty change that all of us seek is not and, even more important, cannot be performed alone. Such change is not solely a matter of willpower and self-control. King Benjamin taught that this change takes place as we yield "to the enticings of the Holy Spirit, and putteth off the natural man and becometh a saint through the atonement of Christ the Lord." He indicated that with the help of Jesus and the Holy Ghost we can become "submissive, meek, humble, patient, full of love," and "willing to submit to all things which the Lord seeth fit to inflict upon" us. (Mosiah 3:19.)

As we change our intentions and the desires of our hearts, we increase our access to God's power and he helps us develop his attributes. Moroni was referring to this assistance when he wrote: "If they humble themselves before me, and have faith in me, then will I make weak things become strong unto them" (Ether 12:27).

Usually this change takes a lifetime. President Ezra Taft Benson warned us: "We must be careful, as we seek to become more and more godlike, that we do not become discouraged and lose hope. Becoming Christlike is a lifetime pursuit and very often involves growth and change that is slow, almost imperceptible." He went on to say that hundreds and thousands of people day by day "move closer to the Lord, little realizing they are building a godlike life. They live quiet lives of goodness, service, and commitment." (*Ensign*, October 1989, p. 5.)

Elder Richard G. Scott emphasized the importance of changing our hearts—our very nature—when he stated, "Righteous character is what you *are*. It is more important than what you own, what you have learned, or what you have accomplished." (*Ensign*, May 1989, p. 37.)

Christ Taught Celestial Attitudes

During his appearance to the Nephites, Jesus delivered a discourse similar to the Sermon on the Mount. In that discourse he taught the significance of inner worship and emphasized the importance of becoming more like him. He replaced some of the old teachings of the law of Moses with a higher law. For example, Jesus declared: "Ye have heard that it hath been said by them of old time [Old Testament prophets], and it is also written before you, that thou shalt not kill . . . but I say unto you, that whosoever is angry with his brother shall be in danger of his judgment" (3 Nephi 12:21–22).

Notice the shift in emphasis from actions to inner feelings that control our actions. This shift makes us responsible not just for what we do but also for what we think and feel and, in fact, for what we really are. Notice this same emphasis in the following two examples taken from this same sermon:

> Behold, it is written by them of old time, that thou shalt not commit adultery;
> But I say unto you, that whosoever looketh on a woman, to lust after her, hath committed adultery already in his heart.
> Behold, I give unto you a commandment, that ye suffer none of these things to enter into your heart. (3 Nephi 12:27–29.)

> And behold it is written also, that thou shalt love thy neighbor and hate thine enemy;
> But behold I say unto you, love your enemies, bless them that curse you, do good to them that hate you, and pray for them who despitefully use you and persecute you;
> That ye may be the children of your Father who is in heaven. (3 Nephi 12:43–45.)

When we make the changes in our soul that Jesus is talking about, we become more celestial and, therefore, more like him and the Father. Jesus points out that this is the whole purpose of the higher law, for he states: "I would that ye should be perfect even as I, or your Father who is in heaven is perfect" (3 Nephi 12:48).

The Pure Love of Christ

According to the scriptures, the most important godlike attribute we need to obtain is charity. Mormon taught that charity is the greatest of all attributes (see Moroni 7:46) and warned us that if we do not have charity, we are nothing (see Moroni 7:44). Since charity is defined as the pure love of Christ, to have charity is to begin to love others as Christ loves them.

In the Greek language, from which the New Testament that we have was translated, there are three separate words for *love*. *Agape* is the word used in the passages in which Christ speaks of love. This is a love for those who have done nothing to deserve our love. It is a love that we are to give unconditionally. This is the kind of love that Jesus demonstrated and is referred to as charity in the scriptures. Mormon described the traits that accompany this love: "And charity suffereth long, and is kind, and envieth not, and is not puffed up, seeketh not her own, is not easily provoked, thinketh no evil, and rejoiceth not in iniquity but rejoiceth in the truth, beareth all things, believeth all things, hopeth all things, endureth all things" (Moroni 7:45).

When we possess this special love we do not give it partially or on certain occasions; rather we share it freely in all circumstances because it has become part of our personality and character. We even love our enemies and are concerned for their welfare. This kind of love is spontaneous. It is not given out of duty or to fulfill some commandment but is a natural expression of the kind of person we have become.

Charity, as with so many other important qualities, is a gift of God. As we do those things that prepare the heart for this great gift, God fills the heart with love. Again, Mormon explained this process as follows: "Wherefore, my beloved brethren, pray unto the Father with all the energy of heart, that ye may be filled with this love, which he hath bestowed upon all who are true followers of his son, Jesus Christ; that ye may become the sons of God; that when he shall appear *we shall be like him*" (Moroni 7:48; emphasis added).

What a wonderful promise this is! As we strive to follow the Savior with all of our energy, our hearts will be filled with the love of Christ, which will make us much more like him. This same principle applies to all godly attributes that we so much desire and need. God's power is activated in our lives as we strive to do his will. When gospel obedience and service spring from love for God and a desire to serve others, the result is always personal spiritual growth.

INDEX

— B —

Bachman, Danel W., missionary experience of, 116

Backman, Robert L., on submission, 58–59

Baptism, covenant of, 75
effect of, 51
symbolism of, 49–50

Benjamin (Nephite prophet-king), on becoming a saint, 47–48, 120
on guilt, 29
Messianic message of, 52–53, 55–57
on mysteries of God, 54

Benson, Ezra Taft, on God's promises, 43
on perfection, 120
on repentance, 45

Bergeson, Nolan, missionary service of, 74–75

Bible, 14

Biddulph, Stephen G., war experience of, 104–5

Blessings, defining, 1
perspective regarding, 1–2, 84
receiving, 2, 4–5, 7
recognizing, 21–22
unearned nature of, 55

Born again, process of being, 47–48, 52, 59
requires commitment, 58–59
through the Atonement, 56–57
See also Baptism

Brown, Hugh B., missionary experience of, 72–73

— C —

Cannon, George Q., on agency, 18–19

Cantwell, Lee G., missionary experience of, 2

Character, 120, 121, 122

Charity, 40–41, 46–47, 121–22
acquisition of, 30–31, 50, 70–71, 84
of Ammon, 73–74, 76
during war, 104–5
of Jesus Christ, 111–12
in missionary work, 76–77

Clarke, J. Richard, on justification for sin, 17

Colclough, Rosetta, missionary experience of, 64–65

Combs, Ned B., 114

Commandments, 46–47, 49

Commitment, to God, 58–59
to missionary service, 74–75
in worship, 87–88

Compassion, of Jesus Christ, 112

Contention, 38

Conversion, 52, 57, 61–62, 64–65, 74–75, 78–79
effects of, 70, 119–20
of Lamanites, 68, 106–7
reasons for, 65
of self, 69
See also Born again

Country, defense of, 101–2

Courage, of Abinadi, 63
of Ammon, 73–74
upon conversion, 71
in missionary work, 72–73

Czenkusch, Alan, climbing experience of, 34

— D —

Disabilities, 21–22, 114–15

Discouragement, patience during, 80–81